Copyright © 2014 The Association for Young Astrologers. All rights reserved.

The Ascendant is the official annual journal of the Association for Young Astrologers. Submission guidelines may be found on our website: www.youngastrologers.org

Executive Editor: Austin Coppock
Editor-in-Chief: Jennifer Zahrt, PhD
Deputy Editor: Nicholas Civitello
Charts Editor: Nick Dagan Best

Layout and Design: Jennifer Zahrt, PhD of Revelore Press
Cover Image: "The Book of the Sun" ©2014 Yuko Ishii

144 limited-edition, signed first copies printed in 2014 by The Association for Young Astrologers. Second printing in 2018 through Revelore Press.

ISBN: 978-1-947544-10-9

The Association for Young Astrologers is a registered 501(c)(3) non-profit organization dedicated to providing educational and networking opportunities for those interested in astrology, with a focus on young people, those new to the field, and aspiring professionals. Our mission is to ensure the continuity of the astrological tradition across generations. To this end we support aspiring astrologers and offer a social networking community where they can learn, be inspired and connect with both peers and mentors. We also publish a yearly journal, offer members access to free educational resources, scholarships to astrology conferences, and more!
Learn more at www.youngastrologers.org

TABLE of CONTENTS

LETTER FROM THE EDITORS ~ 4
*Austin Coppock, Jennifer Zahrt, PhD
& Nicholas Civitello*

An Introduction to Astrological Magic ~ 5
Eric Purdue

Into the Crucible: On the Talismanic Art ~ 10
Tony Bruno Mack

Saturn Returns and Sect ~ 14
Leisa Schaim

What is a Queer Astrology Conference? ~ 20
Ian Waisler

Reflections on a Lost Generation of Queer Astrologers ~ 27
Gary Lorentzen

Astrological Remediation:
An Introduction to Theory and Methodology ~ 33
Andrea L. Gehrz

PHOTOGRAPHY: Venus Envy ~ 38
Wonder Bright

FEATURE:
Cosmos and Chaos:
Perpetual Tides of the Venus-Mars Epoch, Part I ~ 42
Gary P. Caton

INTERACTIVE ART: Astro Orchestra ~ 52
Katie Grinnan

FEATURE:
Human Use of Radioactive Isotopes:
The Problem that Won't Go Away ~ 55
J. Lee Lehman, PhD

The Future of Immersive Astrology ~ 64
Kent Bye

ARTWORK: Constellation ~ 71
Yvette Endrijautzki

☿

Letter from the Editors

Hello, dear reader. While we have your like attention, we'd like to take a second to share with you a glimpse of the process— the 2 years of challenges and decisions otherwise invisible in the finished volume.

Intended to provide a literary outlet for the Association for Young Astrologers, early on we recognized the danger of creating an astrological "kid's table." While there is virtue in providing a literary venue for our younger members, publishing authors on the merit of their age alone is a practice of questionable value. Thus we took great care, from the beginning, to select the finest pieces, irrespective of age. AYA's mission is essentially one of intergenerational continuity, and so while many of the articles contained herein were produced by younger astrologers, this journal includes authors well past Saturn's second return.

There are already a number of astrological organizations publishing astrological journals, and the threat of redundancy hovered over our mission. The challenge, then, was to publish a legitimate addition to the field, rather than a rote replication. In search of uncharted territory we solicited, and received, articles which test the current frontiers of astrological discourse. Some of the pieces extend those boundaries, while others question them, and some plunge far beyond them, seeking both forgotten treasures and wild futures.

Progress is not always a linear thing. Like the orbits of the planets, from our perspective the path twists, turns and doubles back on itself. Thus you may find a going backward, a stumbling and falling into a dusty bed of forgotten texts. Purdue presents the fruit of such library reveries, a keen and scholarly introduction to a nearly lost art, while Mack's piece, the soot-stained, forge-weathered counterpart to Purdue's erudite introduction, reports on the experience of crafting astrological talismans. Together they are theory and praxis, the finest of companions.

Austin Coppock and Jennifer Zahrt wielding the (editorial) trident (Photo: Kaitlin K. Marie Reeves)

The boundaries of astrological knowledge are also tested in more conventional, yet equally powerful, ways. Caton presents new findings on the long cycle of Mars and Venus, and Lehman scrutinizes the potential astrological markers of humanity's perilous relationship to the split atom.

Cultural boundaries are not immune to inquiry, as Lorentzen and Waisler offer penetrating looks at the way sexual culture impacts the work and lives of astrologers. Here Lorentzen reveals the forgotten past while Waisler surveys the future's protean landscape.

Meanwhile, Schaim's thoughtful piece ruptures the antagonistic boundary between the old and the new by applying the ancient doctrine of sect to the modern focus on the Saturn return. Meanwhile, Gehrz' questions the line between divining and creating the future. While many astrologers pay lip-service to the idea of "free will," Gehrz presents a systematic framework for leveraging our agency.

While astrology publications are rarely starved for images, we have included neither the standard classical paintings nor the hypermodern satellite photos which saturate astrological media. Instead, you will find this issue studded with the work of living artists. Astrologer and photographer Bright provides fresh views on Venus, artist Grinnan troubles the boundary between astrology and art, audience and artist, and you'll find many works from the Constellation Art Show, curated by artist Endrijauski, hanging upon our paper walls.

Finally, we close the issue with a tour of the vast possibilities awaiting the art of astrology in the rapidly emerging medium of virtual reality. Here Bye navigates possible futures, cutting pathways into the unknown for us to both walk and dream down.

Welcome to our new journal, we hope you enjoy it.

Austin Coppock,
Jennifer Zahrt, PhD,
&
Nicholas Civitello

An Introduction to Astrological Magic

by Eric Purdue

Since the modern revival of traditional astrology[1] in the 1980s with the rediscovery of William Lilly's *Christian Astrology*,[2] there has been a resurgence of interest, books, courses, and seminars in traditional practices. Most of this material has covered horary, electional, and natal astrology. This is because modern astrology has primarily always focused on natal, electional, and to a lesser extent horary. However in the traditional literature itself, it becomes readily apparent that there is another branch that is largely unstudied today: astrological magic.

There are a few reasons for this, some of which will be discussed later, but the main reason astrological magic is largely unstudied is that, since the nineteenth century, magic and astrology increasingly became separate, if distantly related, entities. This article will hopefully help bridge this apparent gap, show how astrological magic is an integral part of both astrology and magic, and introduce some key concepts, texts, and history to unfamiliar readers.

Where Does Astrological Magic Come From?

As with much of Western metaphysics, astrological magic depends heavily on a medieval Arabic synthesis, and in this case in particular, the magic practiced by the influential Sabaeans of Harran, which is located in modern day southeast Turkey. Beginning in the eighth century, the Sabaeans synthesized a cohesive package of Classical Greek and Roman, Persian, and Hindu magic and astrology, and it is precisely this Sabaean mixture that is the foundation of Western metaphysics. By the late twelfth century, these metaphysical books began to filter back in to Europe, and issued a rebirth of ancient ideas, coupled with newer ideas from the Islamic world.

In astrological magic, much of our information comes from three major sources:

¶ *De Imaginibus* (Of Images) by Thabit ibn Qurra.[3] Thabit was an influential ninth-century Sabaean astronomer/astrologer who is known today as having correctly calculated the length of the year within two seconds of accuracy, and for developing the equation for amicable numbers. *De Imaginibus* is a short work comprised of nine chapters on the construction of astrological talismans for specific effects. His work is quoted almost entirely in *Three Books of Occult Philosophy*.

¶ *Picatrix* (Arabic: *Gayat al-Hakim* or *Goal of the Wise*).[4] The authorship and precise date is uncertain, but most scholars agree that it was originally written in Arabic some time in the tenth or eleventh century, and certainly translated into Latin in the thirteenth. This is without a doubt the main foundation of astrological magic, and provides the specific ceremonies, method, and prayers often missing in Agrippa.

¶ *Three Books of Occult Philosophy* by Heinrich Cornelius Agrippa, 1535. This work is second only to *Picatrix*, but whereas *Picatrix* fills in specific ceremonies, recipes, and prayers, *Three Books* provides the theory behind them, and fleshes out the philosophical aspects that *Picatrix* more briefly touches on. Agrippa attempted to show how magic is not only natural, but also approved by the very ancients and Church fathers Agrippa's contemporaries venerated.

What is Astrological Magic?

In the twenty-first century, astrological magic falls in a gray area between astrology and magic that few modern occultists and astrologers explore in depth. This is a bit less true with occultists, since astrology has always played at least a superficial part, but the in-depth study of astrological magic's particular style of electional astrology is largely missing. In the modern astrological world, focus has shifted more towards chart delineation and psychological study rather than magical work, and for the most part, this shift has been a very deliberate move away from associations with the occult, with its connections with magic and sorcery.

However in the traditional sense, "occult" is much more complex than simply magic and sorcery. Occult comes from the Latin *occultus*, meaning "secret" or "hidden." While magic and sorcery are part of the occult, to a medieval and renaissance reader fluent in Latin, it didn't necessarily only mean those things. It can also refer to the hidden causes and natures of things. The occult, particularly as explained by Agrippa, is the study of numbers, nature, and the celestials, and how they work. Thus, to a medieval academic, magic and astrology are both occult, but astrology by itself is not magic, any more than magic by itself is astrology. But, through understanding the hidden (occult) natures that lie within each of them, both can be enhanced.

To Agrippa and other authorities on magic from the period, the term "astrological magic" is rarely if ever used. It is just "magic." Agrippa defines magic as the uniting of the three worlds—the elemental, celestial, and intellectual.[5]

The elemental world is what we might call nature today. The celestial includes astronomy, astrology, and all mathematics. The intellectual world includes spirits, deities, prayers, and religion. These worlds are not separate from each other, and things that we can perceive (called sensible things in traditional literature) can often straddle two or more worlds, such as the letters of alphabets and sigils include aspects of mathematics and reason.

The *Picatrix* adds that magic is simultaneously the initial premise and conclusion to a full course of knowledge.[6] When a mage "completes" a full study of what amounts to the medieval *trivium* and *quadrivium*,[7] they will find that magic lies at the root of all knowledge.

The astrological portion of magic takes the form of a specialized version of electional astrology. This form of electional is the most important element of the magical ceremony. However electional astrology is only one part of the magical process. Since magic must incorporate many elements, this process has five major components:

1. Philosophical and intellectual understanding
2. Electional astrology
3. Incense and herbs
4. Prayers
5. Talismans

We will discuss each of these components in turn.

Philosophical and Intellectual Understanding

Works

The philosophical foundation of the magic of Agrippa and *Picatrix* is primarily twofold:

⁋ The *Corpus Hermeticum*. This is a collection of 19 short dialogues written in Greek in the late Classical period, though there is speculation that their origin is older and possibly Egyptian. These dialogues are either attributed to Hermes Trismegistus (thrice greatest), or feature Hermes as a teacher in a spiritual and sometimes human form. In addition to these primary texts are several other books and texts attributed to Hermes, the most famous of which is the *Emerald Tablet*, which contains the well-known line "as above, so below."[8] The Hermetica provide the essential framework to the three hermetic arts—magic, astrology, and alchemy.

⁋ Platonism and Neoplatonism. Functionally there is little distinction in magical texts between these two, even though they are separated by over 600 years of development. Core primary texts are Plato's *Timaeus, Republic, Phaedrus*, and others. Some Neoplatonists are Plotinus' *Enneads*, and Iamblichus' *On the Mysteries of the Egyptians*. Plato certainly influenced the Hermetica, as there is much crossover, but whereas the Hermetica can be more technical, Plato and the Neoplatonists are of course philosophical, and expansive where the Hermetica are brief.

In addition to these, Agrippa and *Picatrix* draw on Aristotle, particularly from his *Metaphysics, Meteorology, Physics*, and *On the Heavens*. However, it seems that both Agrippa and *Picatrix* also relied on secondary material and commentaries, particularly from the Arabic Averroes (Ibn Rushd) and Avecenna (Ibn Sina), and in Agrippa's case, Marsilio Ficino's *The Platonic Theology, Three Books on Life*, and Ficino's translations of Proclus.

Basic concepts

Any discussion of the philosophy of planetary magic must begin with what Ficino called the "chain of being."[9] The chain starts at the most superior to the most inferior (as the *Emerald Tablet* says), with each thing being a link in a chain of correspondences and influences. The most superior is God,[10] then the spirits and intelligences, the spheres of the planets, and finally earthly things, which are also called the sublunary world. Each of these links share various qualities. This list is simplified, as there are a vast number of links. We are one link, Jupiter another, and birds another.

This chain works on the idea that inferior things receive influences from their superior. For example, we receive influences from the planets, but planets do not receive influences from us. This is a key to how magic and astrology work according to this worldview. Thus, if you look at the top of the chain, God disposes His influence and will to the spirits, who then dispose to the planets. This influence filters down to the Moon who regulates, and is the final giver of influences, and then these influences spill down to us and anything else in the world.

With this logic, when you conduct magic for a particular planet, the Sun for example, then you must use colors, herbs, prayers, and incense appropriate for the Sun. These would be things like gold, frankincense, cinnamon, verbena, aetite, amber, and so on. These influences also extend to behaviors and certain people, for example Venus influences love, art, and pleasures. Magic with specific planets will enhance, influence, and cause behaviors, people, and natural substances appropriate to that planet because planets belong to a superior link in the chain of being to us.

The chain metaphor goes further. Ficino says that links have three parts: the upper part of a link that connects to the lower part of the one above it, the middle, and the lower part of the link that connects to the upper part of the link below it.[11] The implication here, is that if humans have three parts of the soul, then the upper parts of our soul connects to the lower part of the soul above us in the chain, and the lower parts of our soul connect to the upper parts of the chain below us. This gives an unbroken spiritual link to everything in the universe.

Magic then uses not only the physical correspondences between things, but also the spiritual. Thus our mind and spirit are connected to the mind and spirit associated with the planets and stars, and eventually with God. The goal of magic is not only for making things happen, but also to connect our spirits with the spirit of the divine. This is an important point that is often missed by modern practitioners, and it opens a large area for exploration.

Agrippa mentions that numbers exist in the realm of the Platonic forms,[12] which is to say they are part of the source of being, so numbers are also part of the chain of being, which then connects the technical disciplines of astrology, mathematics, gematria, and sacred geometry, to the nature of the rest of the universe, rather than simply as manmade disciplines. This is true of other non-physical things such as music and alphabets.

Thus everything, whether physical, non-physical, or spiritual, are connected to each other, and by using magic, we are taking an active part in the great machinery of the universe and creation.

Electional Astrology
Basic concepts

Electional astrology is the practice of choosing appropriate times for particular things or events such as marriage dates or the date to start a business. What sets electional astrology apart from natal, is that in natal we take a passive role with astrological influences, but in electional, we take an active role. In astrological magic, the magician chooses appropriate times for when particular astrological points are in their strongest places. The *Picatrix* explains the astrological concepts in more detail than Agrippa, though there is a great deal of overlapping. The most common points used are:

※ Planets – These would be the classical seven planets. Of course the outer planets are not mentioned in traditional literature, but if one chooses to elect for these, their slow motion may make viable elections very sparse.

※ Decans – These are ten degree divisions of the ecliptic, each ruled by a planet. There are two systems of rulership—one following the classical Chaldean order, and another the Hindu triplicity system. In both *Picatrix* and Agrippa, when using the Chaldean order, they are called "fac-

es," and when using the Hindu system, they are called "decans." This distinction is not necessarily consistent in traditional literature. Each face or decan has an effect and image associated with it.

※ Lunar Mansions – These are 28 divisions of the ecliptic, each named after a star. The lunar mansions are analogous in logic to the solar zodiac. Like the decans, lunar mansions have effects and images attributed to them. In Western astrology, unlike Hindu astrology, the mansions seem to have only been used for magic and not for natal or horary.

※ Fixed stars – While there are many stars one can use for magic, the most common stars used for this purpose are the fifteen so-called "Behenian" stars. Each star has an effect(s), stone, incense, and image associated with it.

※ House-based or topic-based talismans – These are some of the most complex elections. Rather than paying attention to the two or so primary points needed for the other types of elections, house-based elections require many points, sometimes three or more, in addition to sometimes requiring specific house placements and aspect configurations. These are fine-tuned to specific goals such as love, business success, money, protection, and so on.

In the simplest elections, the Moon should be unafflicted—that is, not applying to a square or opposition to any planet, particularly Mars and Saturn, and not in fall or detriment. The planet being elected should also be unafflicted, in its ruling or exalted sign, conjunct the ascendant or MC, and in the hour and preferably day of that planet. Fixed star and decan talismans follow a similar logic, but can have some slight differences.

House-based elections must have the rulers of particular houses strengthened by sign and unafflicted, and sometimes even the rulers of the signs those planets are in. These elections often call for a complex network of applying trine and sextile aspects between several planets.

This means that some elections like lunar mansions or fixed stars might be somewhat frequent, but others such as Saturn may not be available for years. Some talismans might not be available more than once or twice in a lifetime. For this reason magicians who practice planetary magic are accustomed to always be looking for possible elections.

Herbs and Incense
Basic concepts

If the philosophical part of magic corresponds to the intellectual world, the astrological part to the celestial world, then herbs, stones, and incense correspond to the natural world. They are in effect the body of the spirit of the planet, or the physical expression of it. Animals also fall under this category, but since the original texts discuss either sacrifice or use parts of animals that might be difficult, illegal, or ethically problematic to obtain today, we will skip this due to practical reasons.

In terms of magical texts, Agrippa has the most extensive list of how and which herbs, trees, flowers, and incense are associated with planets, although *Picatrix* is also valuable. Many non-magical astrological texts give lists of planetary correspondences which can also be helpful. Two notable books are William Lilly's *Christian Astrology*, and al-Biruni's *The Book of Instruction in the Elements of the Art of Astrology*.[13]

One thing to keep in mind is that many natural substances are associated with more than one planet. For example, Agrippa lists hazel for both Jupiter and Mercury, and frankincense, while particularly solar, is used in several blends. There can also be some discrepancies from author to author.

The key to understanding these associations is to understand planetary nature. Agrippa discusses some of this logic, as does Lilly, but it is not too difficult to read between the lines and find some patterns.[14] One must be careful to not take these lists as sole authorities, but guides. This is one reason why we see "discrepancies" from list to list, because the writer is attempting to show the reason behind planetary nature and how to find these natures in anything we may find, regardless of whether they are in a particular list.

Both Agrippa and *Picatrix* have recipes for incense blends. Some are simpler than others, and in most cases mention ingredients that are either illegal or distasteful to use in twenty-first century America. However, again these give you a guide, and it is possible to still make incense blends based on these recipes that are very close by making some substitutions of other appropriate substances. The important thing is to use some kind of appropriate incense during the making of the talisman.

Prayers

The best, and possibly most complete, source of prayers in astrological magic is *Picatrix*, although Agrippa expands on their logic and philosophy. Prayers are uttered with the voice and in effect allow thoughts in the mind to become manifest. During the ritual, this allows the desires of the magician to be known to the spirits.

The close connection between the breath exhaled during speech and spirits is obvious in the Latin and Greek. The Latin for breath *spiritus*, and Greek *pneuma*, also mean spirit. The Egyptian god Ptah, and the god of the Bible created the universe by speaking a word.

The form of the prayers themselves are somewhat open, and the only requirement is that the content of the prayer follow the subject of the ritual and the spirits involved. Some detailed examples can be found in *Picatrix*, and the *Orphic Hymns*. In both examples, the prayers list attributes and sometimes alternate names for the planetary spirits. For example in the Orphic Hymn to Saturn:

> Obstetric Nature, venerable root,
> From which the various forms of being shoot;
> No parts peculiar can thy pow'r enclose,
> Diffus'd thro' all, from which the world arose...[15]

And in the *Picatrix* prayer to Saturn:

> "You are the Lord Saturn, who is cold and dry, dark, advocate of good, truthful in your friendships, truthful in your promises, durable and perservering in your friendships and enmities; your perceptions are far and deep..."[16]

And later:

> "I call upon you by all of your names, which are: in Arabic Zohal, in Latin Saturn, in Persian Keywen, in Roman Koronez, in Greek Hacoronoz, in Indian Sacas..."[17]

These are examples. A prayer from a particular text is not as important as much as a sincere prayer that is appropriate to a particular purpose and spirit.

Talismans

The most common physical result in an astrological magic ritual is a talisman. A talisman collects the essence of the spirit invoked during the ritual, and allows the magician to direct it by keeping the talisman in a particular place, or keep that essence with them by carrying it on their person.

The word "talisman" comes from the Arabic *tlsm*, which according to *Picatrix*, means "violators", because talismans are often made by scratching, engraving, or burning an image into a surface.[18] Talismans are often thought of as amulets, but in reality they can be drawn on paper, sewn, dyed, cast, sculpted, or even a building. However, most astrological elections have a limited time window—often 10–20 minutes—so practical choices are limited.

This brings us to the question of materials. All astrological magic texts describe the materials from which talismans must be made. Sometimes these materials range from the simple and practical such as wax or paper, to the possible but expensive such as gold or silver, to the impractical and dangerous, such as quicksilver or lead. Thabit ibn Qurra gives us a clue to how these materials were practically used, saying that one can use any materials one wishes.[19] Essentially, we should use the stated materials if possible, but sometimes we cannot do this; for example in the cases of quicksilver and lead, they are poisonous. Ficino notes that softer materials tend to have a shorter life than with harder materials, but this does not mean the talisman won't work.[20] Paper talismans can in fact be a good way to introduce oneself to planetary magic due to their impermanence and ease of use.

Putting This All Together

Thus far we have introduced the basic elements of astrological magic. These elements are meant to be used together or in combinations. There are two main approaches to a ritual in astrological magic: Talismanic and Devotional.

These two approaches can be used together or separately, and not all magicians do both. Both have certain things in common.

Talismanic magic

In talismanic magic, the main goal is to produce a physical object with an image that is imbued with the essence of a particular astrological spirit. This talisman will carry over the effects of that spirit and influence the wearer of the talisman or the place that it is kept or buried.

The single most important factor in making a talisman is the astrological timing. While materials, prayers, and incense might vary, if the astrological election is incorrect, the effect of the talisman will either frustrate, or in some cases be contrary to the desires of the magician. The image of the talisman is then created during the window of time where the astrological election is active. This is often a few minutes, but time can vary depending on the election.

In some talismans, such as rings, an herb is incorporated in some way into the talisman. In some sources, a ring talisman is made of a stone with the image facing down, and an herb is placed between the image and the table of a ring, so that the image is hidden and in contact with the herb. In other talismans, herbs can be mixed with molten metal or clay to imbue the substance of the talisman itself.

After the image is made, it is bathed in incense smoke. During this time, prayers are said. *Picatrix* says to say the prayer once and bathe the talisman in smoke, and then prostrate yourself and repeat the prayer several times. You can also meditate during this period.

This is the basic format, but one can also add and personalize this according to one's own traditions, however all of these basic concepts should be included.

Devotional magic

This is not explicitly stated in the traditional texts, but is often done in practice by some magicians. Devotions are completely open, and act as a less formal but more "day-to-day" approach to developing a relationship with the planetary spirits.

One possible approach is to say a daily prayer to the planet ruling the day of the week: the Sun for Sunday, the Moon for Monday, Mars for Tuesday, Mercury for Wednesday, Jupiter for Thursday, Venus for Friday, and Saturn for Saturday. You can burn incense and do a short meditation. This does not require specific astrological elections. Another is to simply meditate daily. The key here is developing a relationship with the planetary spirits so that they can help and interact with us in our daily lives.

Conclusion

The subject of astrological magic is vast and cannot be contained in this short introduction. In horoscopic astrology's roughly 2500-year history, astrological magic has played a prominent role for most of that time. While particular focus has been given to natal astrology, especially since the eighteenth century, astrological magic is a natural part of astrology and cannot be readily dismissed as at least a subject of study. With the study of magic, we can learn more about how the astrological forces work and develop a richer philosophy for our discipline.

☿

Endnotes

1 There is debate on the precise definition of this term. For the purposes of this article, we will define the traditional period as between about the second century BCE to the beginning of the eighteenth century.

2 Olivia Barclay acquired a copy of *Christian Astrology* and reprinted it in a facsimile edition. While this is the common starting point for the resurgence of traditional astrology, other astrologers, particularly Robert Zoller, studied traditional authors since at least the 1970s. See William Lilly, *Christian Astrology* (London, 1647).

3 Thabit ibn Qurra, *De Imaginibus: Astral High Magic, De Imaginibus of Thabit Ibn Qurra*, translated by John Michael Greer and Christopher Warnock (Renaissance Astrology, 2011).

4 Anonymous, *The Picatrix*, translated by Christopher Warnock and John Michael Greer (Adocentyn Press, 2010); See also, *The Picatrix*, translated by Eric Purdue (Private, 2005–2006).

5 Henry Cornelius Agrippa, *Three Books of Occult Philosophy* [TBOP], Translated by Eric Purdue. 3 vols. (Renaissance Astrology, 2012–2015), Book 1: Ch. 2.

6 Anonymous, *Picatrix: Das Ziel Des Weisen Von Pseudo-Magriti*, translated by Hellmut Ritter and Martin Plessner (Warburg Institute, 1962), Book 1, Ch. 1.

7 The *trivium* are grammar, logic, and rhetoric, and the *quadrivium* are arithmetic, music, astronomy, and geometry.

8 The original is "That which is below is as that which is above, and that which is above is as that which is below, to accomplish the wonders of one thing", *Emerald Tablet* line 2. My translation. Chrysogonus Polydorus, ed., "The Emerald Tablet," (n.d.); see also Donald Tyson, ed., "The Emerald Tablet.", in Appendix 1, *Three Books of Occult Philosophy* (Llewellyn, 1993).

9 Marsilio Ficino, *Three Books on Life*, translated by Carol V. Kaske and John R. Clark (Renaissance Society of America, 1998), Book 3, Ch. 4–5.

10 God is not necessarily the god of any particular religion, despite the particular professed religion of the writers. Think of God in terms of the primary source for all things.

"Leo," by Nathan Cartwright, for the Constellation *art show*

11 Marsilio Ficino, *Platonic Theology*, translated by Michael J.B. Allen (Tatti Renaissance Library, 2004), Book 13, Ch. 2.

12 TBOP, Book 3, Ch. 1.

13 See Lilly, *Christian Astrology*; al-Biruni, *The Book of Instruction in the Elements of the Art of Astrology*, translated by R. Ramsay Wright (London: Luzac & Co., 1934).

14 TBOP Book 1, Ch. 7, 22-30; Lilly, *Christian Astrology*, Book 1, Ch. 8–14.

15 Anonymous, *The Orphic Hymns*, translated by Thomas Taylor (1792), hymn XII.

16 *Picatrix*, Book 3, Ch. 7.

17 *Picatrix*, Book 3, Ch. 7.

18 *Picatrix*, Book 1, Ch. 2.

19 Qurra, *De Imaginibus*, p. 7.

20 TBOP, Book 3, Ch. 14.

Eric Purdue specializes in the study, practice, and reconstruction of traditional pre-eighteenth–century horary, natal, and electional astrology and astrological magic. He has studied and practiced astrology and magic for over 25 years, concurrently practicing Afro/Cuban Santeria for fifteen of those years. He was initiated as a santero in 2000, but while not currently active, it has nonetheless helped inform his approach to magic and ceremony. Volume one of Eric's new translation from the Latin of Henry Cornelius Agrippa's *Three Books of Occult Philosophy* is available now on Amazon, and volumes two and three by mid-2015.

Into the Crucible:
On the Talismanic Art

by Tony Bruno Mack

Most student and professional astrologers have likely heard of an astrological talisman, or have at least a general sense of what it intimates. An object—typically a ring or pendant—imbued with, and capable of exerting a specific astrological influence. The primary attribute that constitutes a true astrological talisman is not the form or materials, but the elected moment of its creation and/or consecration. The election should therefore be a time when the astrological conditions are most favorable for the planet, fixed star, etc., whose influence is most suited to the purpose or intent of the talisman. The artist/magus may incorporate into its design various materials, colors, images and symbols corresponding to, or sympathetic with that planetary sphere. Traditionally, a petition is made to the astrological spirit/intelligence/deity; inviting its power and influence into magical operation, and into the talisman. Attempting to explain how these objects function would not be in anyone's best interest. This is a question I don't expect to arrive at any definitive answer to; nor do I necessarily wish to. If astrological magic could be reduced to something completely satisfying to the intellect, it would be of little interest or value to me. I will instead share with you some first-hand experience of what it has been like creating astrological talismans; and a few conclusions I have arrived at based on what I have observed. But first, a little history.

In 2008, I spent a year getting trained in the arts of metalsmithing, gemstone-setting, and the ancient "lost-wax" casting technique at Studio Jewelers Ltd., an affiliate of Temple University in Manhattan. I am currently an independent goldsmith in Williamsport, PA. My acknowledgement of a spiritual reality, and my fascination with various occult and mystery traditions informed my artistic development from the beginning, and it is evident in the work I produce. From an early age I recognized there was a living intelligence, and a spiritual potency present in all things. The quest was on from the beginning to observe and engage in the mysterious relationship of spirit and matter.

After my training in Manhattan I began to hammer away; pouring all of my soul and intent into rings and pendants bearing Egyptian godforms, runes, Greco-Roman deities, and other various spiritual and esoteric symbols and images. To my knowledge, this was the closest thing an artist or craftsman could achieve to a magical talisman. To my mind, all the power lay in the form, images, and symbols and the effect they had on the beholder, both consciously or unconsciously. I found this alone would not satisfy. It became clear to me that something was missing—either from my method, or within myself. They just didn't hum. I was touching something truly transformative. It was at this crossroads I was contacted by astrologer Austin Coppock, who had seen examples of my work, and happened to be looking for someone with my particular 'smithing skills. At this point my knowledge of astrology was relatively minute and scattered. I had a very basic understanding of planets, signs, and aspects, supplemented by what I was able to extract from material relating to alchemy and Hermeticism. I had absolutely no knowledge of astrological talismans, let alone that there was a tradition, a lineage of astrologer-magi performing this very work, stretching back through centuries. This was it—exactly what I had been searching for. From there, my course was set.

The most fascinating, unanticipated aspect of the work is that the entirety of the process takes on the character of, and is shaped by, the planetary influences sympathetic with the talisman. I imagine this would be an obvious expectation for someone who has acquired some experiential knowledge of astrology. After all, every earthly process is unfolding within the context of what the transiting astrology speaks for at any given time. What amazes me about the talismanic work, however, is the degree to which this is taken as each project progresses; a point to which the corresponding sphere's influence becomes undeniable. Each astrological talisman comes with its own lessons, challenges, breakthroughs, and insights unique to that particular planetary intelligence—each its own initiation.

To give you an example, let's examine the experience of creating one of my first astrological talismans: a commission for three planetary rings of Saturn. Now, taking into account what was just explained concerning the initiatory element of each astrological talisman working, and given the nature of Saturn, what do you imagine this experience would have been typified by? If you guessed getting to know intimately my own limitations, need for self-discipline, responsibility, the reality of action and consequence, loss, and reverence, you're solid. On a mundane level, the manual fabrication of the rings alone posed saturnine challenges. The level of technical skill required by its very design and materials meant employing everything I had learned about jewelry and metalworking up to that point. It demanded that I demonstrate a level of concentration, precision, and restraint that went beyond what I had come to expect of myself. There was absolutely no margin for error, and if that meant having to do the same task three to seven times over until it was done right, hey, that's just the way Saturn rolls.

It was the days and months following the initial casting of the rings that the real "getting to know Saturn" period took place. The carving of the wax models, melting and pouring of the metal at the moment of the election, petition to Saturn and suffumigation was complete, but, as I have come to observe, the work is far from over. The ring or amulet itself may as well be cleaned up, put to its finishing touches and sent off to its destined owner. This is all well and good, but the moment you commit yourself to a task of this nature, you are calling upon, and entering into relationship with that aspect of the Divine Intelligence. The corresponding planetary influence will be felt and observed well after the transiting astrology of the election has passed. The obvious and most sincere mode of relating to and co-operating with the planetary spheres in this direct, hands-on, magical context is that of a personal/transpersonal relationship—not as static archetypal abstractions, hovering somewhere "out there", but dynamic, omnipresent, living intelligences. Saturn's influence undoubtedly presided over this period; scales in hand, weighing in on matters from his exalted throne until obligations were met, and the work was complete. Heavy stuff. That being said, I personally would not recommend getting your feet wet in astrological magic with a Saturn talisman.

Tony Bruno Mack in his studio (Photo: Mack)

Countless "on-point" anecdotes accompany these projects, and they are not confined within the perceived context of the project itself. Particular circumstances and encounters will manifest, reflecting near-perfect images of the respective planetary influence, clothed in its various attributes—moments that speak of the reality of astrological influence and correspondence. The planetary rings of Saturn required one precisely pyramid-cut onyx stone each. I searched all possible outlets, contacted every stone dealer and jeweler I knew, to no avail. I was working for an established goldsmith at the time whose father spent a lot of time in the studio. He was an elderly man with a wonderfully sarcastic humor who wouldn't hesitate to give me a word of stern, constructive advice when he saw fit. It occurred to me one day that the machine he spent most of his time working at quietly was a lapidary. This gentleman, probably in his eighties, knew how to cut gemstones. Not only that, he also happened to have a large specimen of raw onyx just underneath his workbench. And so it was from his weathered, tempered hands that the onyx pyramids for the Saturn rings came to be. There could not have been a more perfect image. This is but one of countless instances of a similar nature.

Jupiter's ingress into Cancer (2013) brought with it the first of many ripe elections for Jupiter talismans, it being the first time the greater benefic had been in exaltation or domicile since I started creating astrological talismans. Though I had been creating these objects for a couple years, I had yet to make one for myself. What better time to do just that? The peak of the Jupiter work came about in September, culminating when Jupiter reached its degree of exaltation. I was not certain what to expect out of all the Jupiter work I had been so engaged in, or of my own experience wearing an astrological talisman. One recalls the familiar Jupiter significations and might expect the "Lord of Plenty" to make it rain wealth, wisdom, and all manner of abundance. Soon enough, circumstances had become so that I found myself having little time or energy to consider that question. An increasing number of jewelry and talisman commissions were stacking up, and I began working double the usual hours at a job on the side. I was accomplishing much more than usual, but became so loaded with work that I made little time for sleep. I exhausted my energy to the point that I began to feel physically unwell.

After the majority of my workload was complete, I took a week off both jobs. I hopped on a plane to visit my mother, who lives on an island in the Florida Keys. With time to regenerate and reflect on recent events by the ocean water, I looked into the yellow sapphire of my ring of Jupiter underneath the clear waters of the Gulf. It became clear to me then, the abundance I waited to see brought about by Jupiter had already arrived. It arrived in the form of increased opportunities to work and earn wealth—opportunities to

"Perhaps it was stolen? Of course it was. If it's not here, someone obviously made off with it…but who would I have allowed into my home that would even consider stealing it?" I carried on brooding in this manner for some time. Soon enough I grew tired of myself, and asked why I had started looking for the talisman in the first place. It was then I noticed how identified I had allowed myself to become with the idea of a possession. This particular Mars talisman is a perfect example of why it is so important to have an understanding of, and to observe the rules of traditional/Medieval astrology. To my adolescent astro-knowledge at the time, it seemed sufficient enough for a Mars talisman to have him in domicile, on the midheaven, and with a powerful moon in aspect. Had I looked at the election with my

> **STRONG, MIGHTY VULCAN, BEARING SPLENDID LIGHT,**
> **UNWEARY'D FIRE, WITH FLAMING TORRENTS BRIGHT:**
> **STRONG-HANDED, DEATHLESS, AND OF ART DIVINE,**
> **PURE ELEMENT, A PORTION OF THE WORLD IS THINE**
> —*Orphic Hymn to Vulcan (Hephaestus)*

grow professionally, provide a service, and cultivate abundance. It arrived in the realization that I was in a literal paradise thanks to loving family, and I had everything to be grateful for. The lesson of Jupiter was that I did not temper my hastiness to take on each opportunity as it arose. I overestimated the amount of work I was capable of taking on at one time and managing in a realistic fashion. While walking along the coast with these thoughts in my mind, I spotted the biggest crab I had ever seen. I darted forward and scooped it out of the shallow water, holding its carapace from behind its rear legs. Sure enough, it reached behind and nailed me with its pincer. What realization relating to Jupiter in Cancer had I come to just moments before?

Early on, not long after discovering astrological talismans, I took it upon myself to elect and cast a Mars talisman. Mars had entered its domicile in Scorpio, and I had the most brutally awesome design for a scorpion shaped pendant; adorned with garnet and an iron forged stinger. I had no particular reason to make a Mars talisman, other than to see through the design I had imagined for it. I went through with the election, and it came out looking and feeling as intense as I imagined—excellent. I checked Mars off my list, put the talisman aside and moved on to the next project. Some weeks went by and eventually I went to look for the Mars piece, but I couldn't locate it. I checked every inch of my house and studio three times over, but found nothing. I began to search recklessly, with a growing frustration and anger. By then I had invested too much time and energy to let it go. I was obsessed.

knowledge of astrology today, I might have opted for a trine with Mars in Scorpio and the Moon in Pisces rather than the opposition of Moon in Taurus. I would have noticed that the moon's last aspect was an opposition with Saturn, which means the Moon, though exalted by sign, was besieged by malefics. Not to mention Mars culminating on the MC put Pluto directly on the ascendant. (I do observe Uranus, Neptune, and Pluto in my elections, but I do not consider them to have rulership.)

Paying careful attention to the details of a talisman's astrological election and construction is critical. It is equally important to treat these talismans with respect and not to underestimate their potential or take them for granted. This reminds me of a Venus degree of exaltation talisman I made not long ago. I finished the casting and petition weeks before getting around to wearing it. Within five minutes of me putting on the Venus pendant I was called by my friend (a Libra) to come over, socialize, and enjoy some food. Shortly after that call, I received a text message from a Taurus friend I had not seen in months suggesting we meet for lunch the next day and catch up.

Immersing yourself into said "direct, hands-on" astrological magic is an excellent route to getting familiar with the planetary spheres at an experiential level—to acquire a kind of visceral knowing. I came into astrology and creating astrological talismans through the door of the "Western" magical tradition; through my interest in Hermeticism and alchemy. I consider each talisman completed a step along the path of the "Great Work." Like precious ore heated in the crucible, the student undergoes a process of refinement. Just as, "as above, so below"—the student consciously participates and cooperates with the astrological patterns as they unfold, drawing them into the talisman or magical operation—also, "as within, so without." Not unlike the talisman itself, the student's own awareness and experience become saturated and charged with the very principle he has invoked. He or she is then given the task of stripping away the dross, falsities, projections, and erroneous functioning that would inhibit the final expression of that very principle within himself according to his/her nativity. Examining your natal chart and observing the dignity, debility, and other conditions effecting natal placements can give one a sense of the degree of refinement that must take place. If the student fails to acknowledge and succeed in accomplishing this internal work to reasonable degree, he has at best only managed to exacerbate his own difficulties and complications relating to that planetary sphere, particularly in those houses which the planet has lordship.

This kind of work is not exclusive to Saturn and Mars, I might add. Jupiter and Venus, delicious as they may be, can be just as just as problematic. For instance: Would you be more likely to grow and move out of your current situation into the next phase of your development if you were: (a) reclined on a soft bed with a lover, surrounded by an opulent feast with platters of rich deserts? (b) dropped into a dungeon with a rabid wolf and a skeletal bard who recounts all of your regrets and shortcomings with out-of-tune jigs?

Astrological magic is not always light work, but it has brought with it some of the most insightful, gratifying, awe-inspiring experiences, and it has introduced me to some of the most incredible, intelligent, and beautiful individuals I have had the pleasure of knowing and working with. In a very organic fashion, creating astrological talismans and cultivating a relationship with the planetary spirits has become the dojo of my spiritual practice. It is the most enjoyable and gratifying work I could imagine doing, and I would not trade this craft, or the experiences it has brought with it for anything. I do, however, have a certain responsibility to communicate the reality and magnitude of astrological magic. It is a hidden, yet immediately accessible source of power and transformation. It is exclusive to no one, and has just as much potential to bring about harm as it does to manifest truth, beauty, and a living connection to the world soul.

The aim of the work should be, always and without exception, to help alleviate suffering, to bring about positive and constructive qualities, and to encourage greater knowledge of one's nature and purpose. I would be doing a tremendous disservice to paint a glamorous picture that working with astrological magic has been all 100% awesome. It requires firm dedication to the client, to yourself, and to deity. It means getting up at 4AM to fire up the crucible, anticipating the approaching election. It means reciting Orphic hymns and adorations to Venus as she ascends while holding a 1400 degree mold, clenched in glowing red tongs. It demands precise timing, acute observation of the rules of traditional astrology, and, most importantly, that you are willing to humble yourself, and perform the work with only the most altruistic intentions—not only for the client, but for all those he/she would come in contact with.

The talismanic art is, to my mind, the highest synthesis of spiritual and material art achievable. I believe it has immeasurable potential for application in astrological remediation, and merits the particular consideration of consultation-based astrologers with a regular/repeat clientele. This tradition has again only recently seen the light of day. I expect there will be much more to come out of this beautiful piece of the tradition, as both astrology and the interest in astrological magic gain momentum. It is a sublime art, and to a sincere seeker it offers a legitimate and fruitful spiritual path. If utilized intelligently and with reverence, it is a remarkable tool practicing astrologers can employ to help empower and transform themselves and their clients.

☿

Professional Goldsmith, Metalworker, and artist of various mediums, ANTHONY (TONY) BRUNO MACK received training in jewelry fabrication, advanced stone-setting, and the ancient "lost wax" casting technique at Studio Jewelers Ltd. in Manhattan, NYC, where he graduated in 2008. He has worked as a community artist, muralist, graphic designer/illustrator, and has had his work featured in several publications and art exhibits including the former B&S Gallery, Williamsport, PA. Tony currently works from his studio in central Pennsylvania, specializing in astrological-talismanic jewelry; observing Medieval/Hellenistic astrological techniques, and utilizing traditional metals, gemstones, and design elements in ritual setting. He can be found online at www.facebook.com/Tony.Mack.5 and www.etsy.com/shop/TonyMack.

Saturn & Sect Returns

by Leisa Schaim

Leisa Schaim is a Denver, Colorado-based astrologer with a particular interest in combining the best of both modern and traditional astrological techniques. She has a BA in Interdisciplinary Social Sciences from Antioch College and did graduate work in Religious Studies at the University of Colorado. She is the presiding officer of AFAN, is co-organizer of the Denver Astrology Group, and is a former board member of the Association for Young Astrologers. Leisa can be reached via LeisaSchaim.com, SaturnReturnStories.com, and lschaim@gmail.com.

The Saturn return is a well-known astrological phenomenon, probably the next most commonly recognized astrological term after Sun signs and Mercury retrograde. It takes place approximately every 29.5 years, and lasts roughly 2–3 years, depending on whether it retrogrades back and forth between signs during that time. It tends to be a critical turning point in everyone's life, in some way or another. The Saturn return is often described in one of two manners: as a time of great achievements and pinnacles, and alternately, as a time of great obstacles and difficulty. In this article, I will discuss how we can distinguish more clearly what the quality of an individual's Saturn return will be, and also why it matters that we do so.

Much of the contemporary practice of astrology centers around archetypes and the individual self-will in order to maximize the "good" sides of planetary archetypes and minimize the undesirable ones. Certainly no one would argue that individual effort is not important; however, I am going to assert that there are technical distinctions that explain some of the differences that various people experience with the same transits.

One of the major approaches in contemporary astrology regarding the Saturn return is encapsulated in the phrase, "do the work." There is an idea that since Saturn tends to be about hard work, then if you do whatever Saturn "wants" from you, you will have good results in the end. However, I believe that this model, although perhaps true some of the time, is problematic if uniformly applied to all lives and charts. I would like to introduce the idea of sect as a major distinction in how people experience their Saturn return. First, though, we should take a look at what Saturn signifies in itself.

It is often useful to return to the root meanings of a topic under consideration, even if one feels familiar with the topic already, in order to consider the issue anew. Vettius Valens, in the second century wrote this about the nature of Saturn: "[Saturn] makes...constrictions, bonds, griefs, accusations, tears, cases of orphanhood, captivities, exposures...It procures great reputation and notable rank, guardianships and the administration of the affairs of others..."[1] These sound like two distinctly different energies: the first grouping describes generally difficult and painful experiences, while the second lists positive and admirable events.

If we jump ahead to modern descriptions of Saturn, we find that the depiction has actually stayed virtually the same. Richard Tarnas, in his comprehensive 2006 book Cosmos

...THE EXPERIENCES THAT DIFFERENT PEOPLE GO THROUGH DURING THEIR RESPECTIVE SATURN RETURNS ROUGHLY LINE UP ACCORDING TO THE SECT STATUS OF THE CHART.

and Psyche, describes the nature of Saturn this way: "To experience difficulty, decline, deprivation, defect and deficit, defeat, failure, loss, alienation, the labor of existence, suffering, old age, death...restraint and patience, endurance, responsibility, seriousness, authority, wisdom."[2] This is again a great spectrum, the first grouping in this excerpt listing experiences that all describe a lack of some sort, while the second group describes what we would think of as positive Saturnian qualities.

A technical distinction actually already exists in the astrological tradition that can speak to some of these disparate specifics—sect. Sect is a Hellenistic astrological concept that describes how planets behave differently in charts depending on whether one is born during the day or at night. The sect of the chart is determined by whether the Sun is above or below the ascendant/descendant axis: if above, it is a day chart, while if below, it is a night chart.

The sect status of a chart divides up the classical planets into two groups. The planets that belong to the diurnal sect are the Sun, Jupiter, and Saturn, while the nocturnal sect claims the Moon, Venus, and Mars. Mercury is neutral and can be considered to belong to one sect over the other depending on other chart factors.

Each of these planetary groupings is composed of one luminary, one benefic planet and one malefic planet. The so-called "benefic" planets, Jupiter and Venus, are considered such because of their power to affirm or to improve certain topics, while the so-called "malefic" planets, Saturn and Mars, have the power to deny or harm certain topics. Two common objections should be immediately addressed before proceeding further. The language used here is merely signifying the state of a topic being improved or made more difficult; this should not be read as the planet actually acting, but is merely a useful shorthand way of speaking about it. It is also worth mentioning that this is not referring to an individual person being bad or good, but rather to certain external topics in one's life being improved or made more difficult.

Sect modifies the qualitative status of these planets, particularly the benefic and malefic planets, so that they are more beneficial or harmful in different charts. So referring to the two groupings mentioned earlier, the planet Saturn is more constructive and positive in day charts, while it is more harmful and negative in night charts. Mars is the opposite, so that in night charts it is more constructive, while in day charts it is more harmful. The benefic planets, Jupiter and Venus, follow the same pattern, so that in day charts Jupiter is more helpful, while in night charts it is less so; Venus is more beneficial in night charts, while less so in day charts.

Going forward we will focus mostly on how this modifies Saturn in the charts of people born during the day or at night. So in day charts, Saturn tends to exhibit its more constructive qualities, such as responsibility, hard work leading to success or acclaim, etc. The night charts, conversely, tend to exhibit the less desirable qualities and situations associated with Saturn, such as loss and suffering. There are some other factors that modify this basic distinction, but sect is one major factor in how Saturn will be experienced in a given chart.

Following from this distinction, then, the experiences that different people go through during their respective Saturn returns roughly line up according to the sect status of the chart. Since at the Saturn return, the qualities and placement of Saturn in the chart are intensified and highlighted, then whatever its basic nature is in the natal chart will become even more apparent.

I would recommend using whole sign houses as the primary house system in evaluating this for now, and using a quadrant house system as secondary if that is what you normally use. The whole sign house system was the original house system in use when the concept of sect was developed, so it is important to use them together in order to most fairly evaluate how this is working in charts. I would also recommend using the classical rulerships with this concept for the same reason, as well as whole sign aspects, meaning that all Ptolemaic aspects by sign rather than degree are operating.

The following are some chart examples illustrating how sect is observable in real peoples' charts and life events.

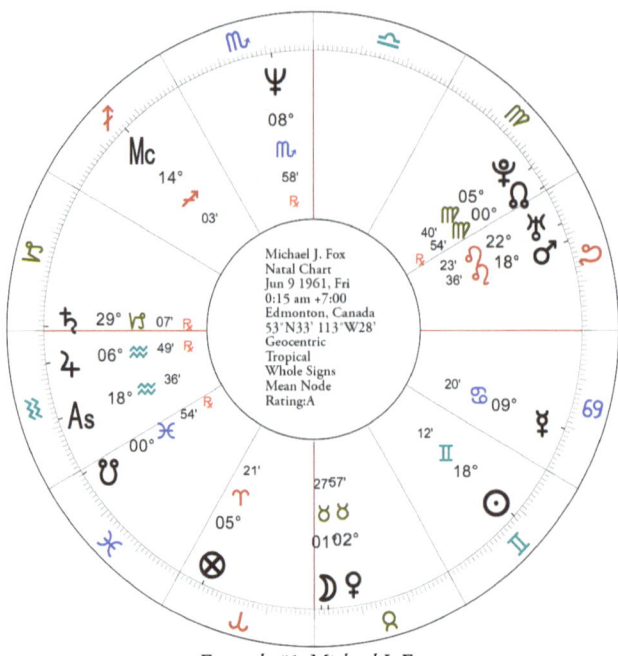
Example #1: Michael J. Fox

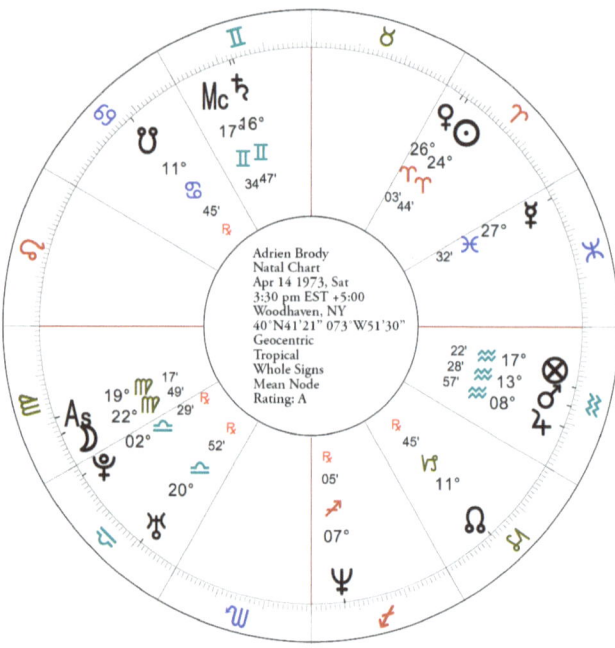
Example chart #2: Adrien Brody

❡ EXAMPLE #1: Michael J. Fox (June 9, 1961, 12:15AM. Edmonton, Alberta, Canada). Michael J. Fox has the Sun below the ascendant/descendant axis in Gemini, so he has a night chart. This will mean that his Saturn has some of the less desirable qualities associated with it. His chart has Aquarius rising, with Saturn ruling both the 1st and the 12th houses and placed in the 12th house in Capricorn. Since Saturn is ruling the 1st house of the body and the primary house signifying the native and is in the 12th house, as well as is of the night sect, we can expect that his Saturn return would possibly have something to do with the body, as well as something with some of the negative Saturnian qualities like loss or suffering. At his Saturn return, Michael J. Fox was diagnosed with Parkinson's disease, a currently incurable chronic illness that led to his eventual need to stop his successful full-time acting career. It is notable that he had been working at this vocation from a young age.

❡ EXAMPLE #2: Adrien Brody (April 14, 1973, 3:30PM. Woodhaven, New York). Adrien Brody has the Sun above the ascendant/descendant axis in Aries, so he has a day chart. This will mean that his Saturn will have some of the more constructive qualities associated with it. His chart has Virgo rising, with Saturn ruling the 5th and 6th houses and placed in the 10th house in Gemini. We would expect his Saturn return to be focused on career (10th house), which was somehow related to the topics of the 5th house (creative expression or children) and/or the 6th house (health, bodily habits, work), as well as express some of the more positive Saturnian qualities like work leading to success. At his Saturn return, Adrien Brody became the youngest person to ever win the Academy Award for Best Actor for his role in the film *The Pianist*. To successfully portray his character in this film, a pianist who lived through and survived the Holocaust, Brody purposely lost a lot of weight, withdrew from society, and gave up his apartment and car—certainly Saturnian experiences, but both reversible and purposely taken on, that led to his major success in the end.

❡ EXAMPLE #3: Anonymous (September 28, 1979, 11:09AM. Sitka, Alaska). This native has the Sun above the ascendant/descendant axis in Libra, so she has a day chart. Her Saturn is in the 11th house, and rules the 3rd and 4th houses. We would expect then that her Saturn return would have something to do with the topics of friends or groups/associations (11th house), siblings or communications (3rd house) and the home or family (4th house). Given that this is a day chart, we would also expect these topics to exhibit more of the positive Saturnian characteristics. During her Saturn return, she started a business leadership group for young women. She also bought her first house, and reconnected with a half-sibling that she had previously known about but not talked with much, which she reported has continued to be a positive relationship in her life.

❡ EXAMPLE #4: Anonymous (October 21, 1955, 9:48PM. Denver, Colorado). This native has the Sun below the ascendant/descendant axis in Libra, so he has a night chart. His Saturn is in the 5th house, and rules the 7th and 8th houses. We would expect that his Saturn return would have something to do with the topics of children or sexuality (5th house), partnership (7th house), and/or death (8th house). As his Saturn return began, he got into a relationship with a woman, who became pregnant but then quickly disappeared from the area, so he never knew if she had the child or not. He also got married himself later in his Saturn return, but they divorced after only about two years. His stepfather, whom he was fond of, also died during his Saturn return.

¶ EXAMPLE #5: Anonymous (April 12, 1980, 2:48 pm. Brooklyn, New York). This native has the Sun above the ascendant/descendant axis in Aries, so she has a day chart. Her Saturn is in the 1st house, and rules the 5th and 6th houses. We would expect that her Saturn return would involve the topics of body or general self (1st house), as well as possibly recreation or children (5th house) and/or bodily habits or work (6th house). She had been abusing alcohol and drugs for close to ten years, and at her Saturn return decided to become sober and successfully did so. She also started receiving body-centered therapy, and found that to be such a helpful experience that she eventually went back to school to become a counselor herself.

I HOPE THAT THESE examples start to show some of the general differences between day and night charts at the Saturn return. In the day chart examples, the natives here tended to have more overall positive experiences that included some sort of success or attainment of a life goal, or an overcoming of a previous difficulty. The night charts tended to have a difficulty crop up during the Saturn return that involved something outside of the native's control, either another person or a serious illness.

The sect status of one's Saturn is one major distinction for how to interpret the probable quality of a given Saturn return, but it does not stand alone. Briefly, some of the other factors that alter this basic distinction include whole-sign aspects from the benefic planets Jupiter or Venus, especially by superior trine or square; Saturn being in its own sign or exaltation, and aspects from the other malefic planet Mars, especially hard aspects. In this way, we can see some of the gradations of experience that happen in real peoples' lives depicted using these factors.

So, now that we have gone though the technical manner in which Saturn returns are affected by sect, I would like

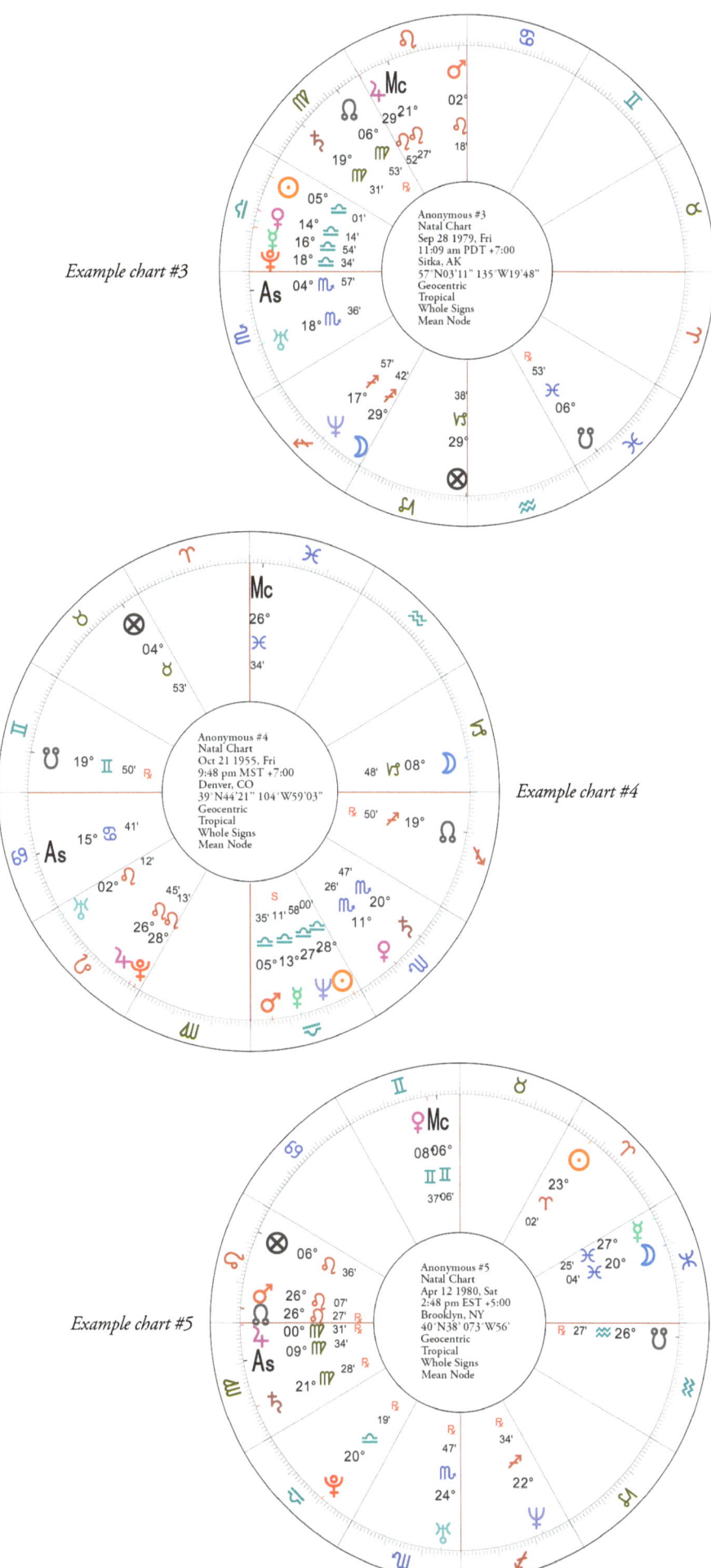

Example chart #3

Example chart #4

Example chart #5

to explain two major reasons this seems important. The first reason is accuracy: we can simply gain a more specific understanding of what someone's experience will be or has been, which should be reason enough to care about this in a field focused on knowing things we should not otherwise be able to know about another person's life. In particular, seeing the myriad ways in which Saturn returns can manifest in either some of the more constructive or the more difficult experiences on the Saturnian spectrum and how that correlates with sect can inform our practice of astrology.

One of the things this shows us is that some Saturn return experiences more closely conform to the "reap what you sow" aphorism, but not all. The first two example charts shown earlier are a nice study in contrast with respect to this. Adrien Brody is a near-perfect example of this typical way of thinking about the Saturn return: he put in an enormous amount of effort getting prepared for his role in *The Pianist*, and then it all was rewarded in the end with great success and a career peak. But some difficulties also come unbidden through no fault of one's own, no matter how hard one is working: Michael J. Fox had been working since age fifteen as an actor and had already had great success, but nonetheless he developed a debilitating chronic illness at his Saturn return that severely limited his career from that point forward.

A common objection that is frequently raised to this kind of thinking is that there isn't really any objectively "bad" or "good experience," but that instead what is most important is how one thinks about it or works with it internally, either psychologically or spiritually. My first response to this is that there are still specific life events that are generally more or less desirable to real people, and being able to identify those is a first step in talking about them if one is an astrologer and not only a counselor. My second response would be that such a perspective can be received as quite insensitive by someone who has experienced objectively difficult external life events, and that one must start with what has actually happened before going anywhere else with it. Now, what one does with the difficulty is a different matter. I think you can usefully ask in almost any circumstance, "what can I learn from this," but it is a denial of reality not to admit that some situations are much harder than others.

The second major reason I think this sect distinction is important is compassion. The downside of a pure empowerment approach to astrology is blame for all of the difficulties one experiences. Occasionally someone will actually say that explicitly, but most often it is just unavoidably implicit if you suggest to your clients that all their results are based on the effort they put in. I think this is a problem when we are in the position as astrologers of interpreting individuals' lives and claiming to know more about their overall plan and timing than someone should otherwise know. This puts us in a kind of quasi-religious position, which has the potential to make implicit blame that much more harmful. Especially because we are often so good at saying the "what" of what is going on in someone's life and having it line up with the person's actual experience, they are a lot more likely to believe us if we say or even imply, "and this is why."

It is understandable that most astrologers would want to speak to things that are under the native's control, because that is the only thing one's own self-will can have any effect on. My concern is that an astrology that implies it is all up to self-will excludes a great number of people in the world, anyone who has had any major life difficulty unrelated to their own actions. Without the tool of sect, it is easy to see some people thriving during their Saturn return and some people suffering, and to chalk it all up to their disparate free will choices.

One of Saturn's traditional significations is wisdom. In contrast with the Jupiterian wisdom of the exuberant preacher or prophet, Saturnian wisdom is borne of sober, realistic experience over time. This is the kind of wisdom associated with archetype of the wise old elder, who has been around for a long time and has seen how life works. That is why we value their wisdom: they have lived long enough to see both good and bad times and have gained proper perspective from that. True wisdom is the kind that understands that life contains both opportunities that you can only grasp through hard work and difficulties outside of our individual control. We can be better astrologers if we can first see these distinctions in charts, and can also compassionately communicate with our clients or to others through our public writing and speaking, no matter where they may happen to fall on that spectrum of life experiences.

As astrologers, we assume the role of dispensing wisdom. I have the hope that we can be like that wise old elder, no matter our age, to truly be able to see and validate the entire spectrum of life experiences. Incorporating sect into our delineations is an important tool in achieving the ability to show why some experiences will go more positively or negatively in different people's lives. Ultimately, if what we are interpreting is life itself, that by definition must include the light and the dark, the wondrous and the devastating. We can work with what happens internally, but that need not conflict with acknowledging the quality of external events themselves. By being both able and willing to see these distinctions in people's charts and lives, we can serve as clear-eyed, compassionate witnesses to reality.

Endnotes

1 Vettius Valens, *The Anthology: Book I*, trans. Robert Schmidt (Berkeley Springs: Golden Hind Press, 1993), p. 2.

2 Richard Tarnas, *Cosmos and Psyche*, (New York: Viking, 2006), p. 91.

"Saturn's Children," embroidery by S. L. Baumgart, for the CONSTELLATION art show

*Saturn's Children are symbols of Himself and the wards of Night's Black Agents upon the sublunary sphere of earth.
These flora and fauna of the Old Dark Lord are here represented by two poison plants of the Nightshade family:
hellebore, renowned as both fatal toxin and ingredient in the witch's unguent,
and bittersweet nightshade, whose very name implies its nature.
The Guard-Tree of Blackthorn gives its blessing and curse upon the living, for knowledge of life is death.
A shield of thyme mixes a Saturnian play on words as well as sweetens the blow of age, being loved by Venus in turn.
The Death's Head moth below the sign of Saturnus is the Master's emissary upon earth—an omen of love and demise.*

What is a Queer Astrology Conference?
by Ian Waisler

What do you mean, Queer?

In her account of the first Queer Astrology Conference, in *The Mountain Astrologer*, astrologer Erin D'Estrée wrote of the descriptor *genderqueer*: "This category is willfully unstable."[1] As I continue to relate to the open question: What is Queer Astrology?, a conscious engagement with this type of instability generates better questions and an ever broadening range of interpretation.

The word *queer* has complicated reference. The historical and spectral contexts of its usage are well documented. If your circumstances have shielded you from a direct encounter with queerness, kindly consider that in this historical moment it denotes a provocation of so-called *normal* which can no longer be repressed. This is at least how I am using it. As astrologers I trust our common experience equips us to handle such a versatile word and dynamic process with more openness than those uninitiated in our art. And as a group of practitioners who are already pressed to stabilize ourselves in the face of both religious and scientific critiques, we know well the arc of coming out.

Too much of the discussion I've noticed on the questions of a queer astrology reduces the inquiry to concerns specific to sexual preference; these are more appropriately denoted by words like lesbian or gay. These miss the point. For sure, the experience of transfolk brings new questions which have just barely been represented in astrological literature. And all manner of hidden and taboo headlines will always sell tickets. While these fields of inquiry are rich, they are too narrow and miss the possibilities inherent in the meme: Queer Astrology.

Consider another ubiquitous saying as a useful frame: "Not gay as in happy, but queer as in fuck you." Rather than emphasize the elusive authorship of this quote, I choose to point to the way this quote has traveled namelessly into the collective. While the first Queer Astrology Conference was hosted in an academic setting, presentations moved easily among the well-cited and researched scholastic, and spontaneous creativity, artistry, mystery. When working in a theme about which there is little documented history, we must exploit the freedom of exploring where our questions lead.

Queering includes the deconstruction of text inclusive of a reader's awareness of specific cultural origin and author's bias. The legacy of astrological texts of course reflects the enduring cultures where they originate. While for some an astrology strictly steeped in ancient tradition holds sway, for others, an astrology relevant and responsive to evolving experiences must reflect and incorporate diversity and expansions in how we identify ourselves. Among its many facets, Queer Astrology calls us to the very edges where our axial beliefs can no longer hold. But rather than simply shattering them, we gather to encounter how rupture is necessary to reveal undreamed of terrain.

The Queer Astrology Conference held in San Francisco in July 2013 arose directly from a shared experience of these directions being absent at the 2012 United Astrology Conference in New Orleans. A group of us peers organically constellated an actual experiment, inquiring what we had to say, and how it might be of use to our peers. In telling the stories of how we met, how the event was organized, and what comes next, I hope to inspire ever more bold astrological exploration.

United Astrology Conference, New Orleans; Meeting the Family

While I had never heard the call to a national conference, not yet awake to the merits of long sunless days in hotel ballrooms, the United Astrology Conference kept tapping my psychic shoulder. For those of you who are not familiar with it, UAC is giant. Sixteen concurrent speaker panels run through four and a half days. Two-thirds of all the well-known living astrologers you have ever wanted to meet are there. Constant decisions between a known speaker and a topic that sounds mind blowing, but is as often as not somewhat obtuse. Also, how many mind-blowing talks can one take on any given day?

At lunch the first day, scanning the crowd in the lobby, my gay-dar lights up on someone who strikes me as signaling a familiar vibe. When I see him in a lecture that afternoon I sit down and say Hello. This is Barry (Perlman), a.k.a. astrobarry. After the lecture, he and his buddy Ben Commons and I struck up a conversation. Barry is indeed a homo, and also from San Francisco; we have lots in common. Ben too, awesome, not queer-identified as such but down with our in-joking; Ben is wickedly funny and smart. I recall us marking our generation of Pluto/Libras, and how the Pluto/Leos are presenting on a wave-length which does not necessarily resonate with us. Fair enough.

The next day, I head to a talk by Geoffrey Cornelius. For some reason it has been moved from the usual conference halls to a room on the thirtieth floor. While waiting for the elevators, which happen to have this security interface which makes them highly unintuitive to a point of uselessness, the irony and our powerlessness helps break the ice among us. A woman with an impossibly gorgeous smile in the elevator next to me says: "I like your headband." (You can take Ian out of San Francisco, but a little queer-marking drag is going to travel with me ... *"Lest anyone mistake me for straight"* as Harry Hay is misquoted as saying.)

My kerchief had caught the eye of none other than Chani Nicholas who filled out the quartet with Barry and Ben and I for the remainder of the conference. Fast friends, we would catch up at least twice daily and trade notes and share inspirations. The Cornelius talk, by the way, was a high point of the conference for me. Entitled "Juice" he spoke on the nature of the energy that elevates a reading out from the usual. Where does it come from? How can we court it? I highly recommend the recording if you can access it.

Day four now, I venture into the bookstore. I happen into Erica Jones. Flashback to the preceding November: a friend enrolled at CIIS (California Institute of Integral Studies, a university in San Francisco) let me know the on-campus astrology group was hosting Carolyn Casey. I was turned on by the lecture, but especially to have found a vein of young astrologers meeting and studying in SF. Erica tells me that she has just graduated and asks me if I know anyone at CIIS who might like to take over the club she had built over several years. Fond of thinking of myself as a matchmaker (*from the Yiddish: yenta*) I tell her I am sure I can find someone.

Queer Astrology calls us to the very edges where our axial beliefs can no longer hold. But rather than simply shattering them, we gather to encounter how rupture is necessary to reveal undreamed of terrain.

Chani and Barry and I, all queer-identified Californians, begin to discuss how, among all the brilliance and amazement on offer, that somehow the whole conference was still couched in what read for us as archaic assumptions. Cultural defaults of gender-binary, a void of attention to class, generally little acknowledgment of the world beyond the Euro-centric...all of this begged our attention. We were not so much critical of UAC, rather we found ourselves called to engage certain spaces we hoped to see diversified. We were called alive by our presence to these questions, which we imagined might be part of our mission in this life. On that very trip Chani confirmed her decision to move from LA to San Francisco; the three of us would have lunch in the fall.

Back in San Francisco, Gathering the Threads

Later that summer (noticing incoming transits in my 3rd, 9th, and to my Jupiter) it finally seemed the right time to enroll at CIIS. It was not so much a conscious choice as a deeper instinctive knowing that it would further develop my calling to work in astrology. CIIS is a hub for local astrologers, with Rick Tarnas and Greg Bogart among the faculty. A few weeks later I was on my way to orientation. I dropped a line to Erica Jones and told her that, surprisingly, I had enrolled and would happily take over the astrologers club: Coniunctio.

Chani and Barry and I met up a few times that fall, with Clare Martin (a friend who was on the SF Astrological Society board) joining us for dinner at mine in December. Clare shared that on the SFAS mailing list there was dialogue about creating an event to commemorate the passing of Jack Fertig. Jack was a very well loved and respected astrologer, and had been a leader with the Sisters of Perpetual Indulgence during the AIDS epidemic. Christopher Renstrom had suggested there ought to be some memorial and presentations at the intersection of gay and astrology. Again an instinctive tug at my belly hollered: get involved with this project.

In January 2013, I set up a meeting with Linea Van Horn, president of the SFAS since its inception twenty years earlier. I asked her what plans were in motion; she said there was nothing more than the idea. She wondered if Coniunctio might supply a venue on the university campus, while SFAS would offer funding and support the program. She sent an email introducing me to Christopher, and also Jessica Lanyadoo to solicit their participation. Jessica and I met for brunch soon after and hit it off swimmingly; she made very clear she was able to consult and help guide the formation of this project. Christopher too was categorically on board for whatever was transpiring. My wheels were turning.

In February I spoke with the dean and assistant dean to explore the possibilities. Student clubs were welcome to host events on campus so long as they were free to students and the public. I was however clear that the event that was gestating wanted a bigger sandbox than this; it needed a cash flow. There were several meetings and email exchanges where I outlined the vision. I was met with both enthusiasm and standard replies welcoming me to host a free event. When I finally revealed that I was eager to run a ticketed event, it was suggested that if my department chair would sign off on the event, it might be possible.

I was having regular lunch dates these days with another dear friend, also an astrologer, Stella Lawson. She had just branded her consulting website Stella the Good Witch. I shared with her first the name that was brewing: Queer Astrology Conference. Although she had basically sworn off organizing after burning out in her college days, she was enthusiastic about joining in. She too felt it in her bones. I could not have asked for a better co-instigator.

Over a long weekend in February, I went on retreat to a radical faerie gathering in central Oregon. The very first evening I was soaking in hot springs with a friend of several years, Brad Colby—Sister Merry Peter of the Sisters of Perpetual Indulgence. I shared the vision, and he immediately offered unconditional support. At the next SPI board meeting he got approval for the event to be sponsored by the Sisters, and offered seed money as well as his advisory ear. The potential of this event resonated everywhere I shared it.

The next week, Barry and Clare came over for dinner, and I said we ought to elect a date. Barry, more instinctually than technically, proposed the grand water trine at the end of July. He imagined it would be a rich time for astrologers to gather. I called up a chart and it read as a powerful confluence. Cast for noon, I did not see that Mercury was stationing direct in the eleven o'clock hour. I didn't discover this until a couple of weeks later.

I met in person with the chair of my department and pitched the event, now validated with sponsorships from SPI and SFAS. He was extremely amenable, specifically adding vision for how it would further my academic plans. When I asked for help booking the rooms, he referred me to the existing channels for doing a free event. (*Ack!*) I reiterated, he paused, then conceded. Gentle insistence garnered his approval to host the now burgeoning conference, with ticketed admission, at least enough to pay honoraria to speakers and afford decent quality documentation.

I headed directly from his office to the Dean and asked if she could help me reserve the rooms on campus. She phoned the registrar's office to make the request, and was told the summer calendar would not be open until the last of April. This would not do. I was disheartened as it would be impossible to plan an event for July without securing the venue until late April.

But one more boon awaited. I wandered into the office of the assistant dean, a student who I had become friendly with in my efforts running Coniunctio. I shared account of the setback, commiserating and venting frustration. She been tracking my scheming, and, being also the advisor for another club at CIIS, was deeply curious to see what might happen. She had me pause, picked up her phone and, ringing the same person in the registrar's office, got a Yes. Queer Astrology Conference was confirmed.

Coming Out

International Astrology Day happens at Spring Equinox.[2] Aware that this would be an ideal event to announce QAC, I got busy. I found an alchemical image of a three-faced, bare-breasted, serpent-tailed being, holding the sun and moon, luckily in the public domain. This has come to be known as the Merperson. I registered queerastrology.com, built a simple site using Wordpress, and published a call:

We call professional and novice astrologers to come together to explore the intersections of study/practice and queer-identified life. By queer, we invite a broadly imagined array of gender and sexual diversity, self-defined identities and lived experiences.

The intent is to work smarter in the present and to generate queer-specific resources for future astrologers. Through sharing audio, video, and written record of the proceedings, we hope to further the research, scholarship, and practice of astrology relevant to ourselves as queer people.

I posted the date and a call for presenters and asked everyone I knew to share it broadly among their communities.

I also handed out a postcard, which we hand-carried to several west coast astrology communities by participants that very weekend. The enthusiasm which met this as-of-yet unformed event was electric. The next week I wrote out a bare bones schedule:

¶ Aries: broadcast the call, build relationships, teams, technological infrastructure
¶ Taurus: plan and publish the schedule, open registration
¶ Gemini: manage registration and strategize on-site logistics
¶ Cancer: carry this event into a fertile living community of teachers and learners
¶ Leo: edit and distribute documents from this conference
¶ Virgo: rest

Aries

I called an open meeting for potential organizers. A week later Stella, Chani, Clare, Erin (another SFAS board member), Lucien (a friend of Chani's) came 'round to strategize. The first go-round was overflowing with ideas which confronted every possible recognizable element of a conference—fun to suggest and nearly impossible to execute. I named myself as Saturnal to a room full of Uranians, committing to hold a degree of structural vision to make sure that by July there would in fact be an event worthy of all the attention the idea garnered.

As far as commitments, Stella and Lu were keen on fundraising so that we might offer scholarships to enable maximum access. Erin took on hospitality, Chani publicity. Clare admitted within a few days that while in deep support of the project, her workaday life demanded she not take on a role. I became *de facto* Speaker Liaison and Registrar. Erin sent me a template of a budget which, with a few tweaks, did wonders in guiding the planning and management of money in and out.

Taurus

Things moved fast. Over the next six weeks, I collected submissions from twelve individuals. I gathered from Barry and Jessica that they might rather discuss their work as consulting astrologers, rather than plan a lecture, so I suggested they collaborate. They became fast friends and were very thrilled to speak together. Erica reached out to her academic colleague Rod O'Neal. Stella invited a writer/speaker she admires named Yolo Akili. Via my friend Jaysen Pluto I got in touch with Rhea Wolf. Lilia found the call on the CIIS mailing list. And, just after I had closed the gate for submissions, we got an inquiry from Eric Francis Coppolino, via the SFAS publicity. The centerpiece of the event remained the evening tribute to Jack, which the Sisters were on board to run. Although it was more events than I had originally envisioned, somehow saying Yes to everyone seemed the truest way forward.

Meanwhile Stella, Chani and Lu, drawing on their social justice backgrounds, proposed that we create caucus spaces. These would be facilitated spaces that would focus on gender and race where participants could unpack their experiences. I had some resistance as these spaces would not be documented and were outside my experience. Certainly many of our feathers got ruffled in the process of working this in, but I am so grateful for their dedication and vision to this part of the program.

Many arrived at the first meeting presuming that any queer-titled project would be collectively run with a consensus-driven process. Given the two months of prep work that I had already contributed, and the chaotic feeling of this first gathering of people, some of whom I was just meeting, I was reticent. I wanted, and certainly needed, collaborators but was not prepared to let go of the reins I was already holding without clarity about how exactly everyone believed this would run. I returned that if anyone wanted to make clear a proposal of a model, to bring it to the next meeting, including what level of decision and ownership people felt they needed at this stage. While we dialogued about it a few weeks later, this situation did not bear out anything concrete. I added "Libra: discuss an organizational structure" to our bulleted planning schedule.

Stella and Lu worked on scripting and producing the video for our fundraising campaign. Around Mayday we gathered at my house with Stella's partner Kay donating his time and equipment, Stella providing the craft services, i.e., dinner. Parenthetically, throughout the journey I noticed some of us exhibiting our rather lunar orientations to what details we prize: meeting over meals for example, while other colleagues clearly show up primarily from their strong Saturns, having built empires of their consulting and writing careers. It has been joyous to see how all our dimensions, not just these, fed one another, and contribute to a well-rounded community, ahead of simple productivity.

This video shoot took place at the entry of eclipse season, and was tumultuous personally and communally to say the least; we encountered several differences of opinion. One of the more dynamic ones to record was the interplay among a queer rejection of any establishment values (*Let's wear crazy costumes!*) scrubbing against our desire for a coherent product which would command the dollars we were calling for. We did agree to play with drag, yet also signal some legible maturity to our peer groups.

Gemini

The delights and ease of running an event in the information age cannot be underestimated. With spreadsheets in the cloud I was working from everywhere; with free Wordpress hosting the public interface was tidy and easily updated. The website was the most concrete form of the event through these months, being the clearinghouse for plans laid and decisions made. Tickets were pre-paid online, the donation platform spread through social media; the ground was laid.

Stephanie Gailing, whom I had met at IAD, had offered any support I might be able to ask of her. She performed a thorough review of all the text on all the sites, queerastrology.com, the fundraising site, and the ticket buying site, and provided a coherent set-up, edits, and clarifications. As you may imagine, steeped as I was in the stew of an event being anchored by words, having her fresh set of eyes to comb and cull the words was a huge gift. With a schedule, blog posts, and FAQs set in place, we opened registration the last week of May.

I got a call from a friend who is assistant to the CIIS President, saying there had been some talk about the event in his office and to be prepared for some news. I got a call from the Dean a few days later who needed to speak with me. *Deep breath...* She told me I needed to remove the name CIIS from any of the promotional material and to excise their name as a sponsor of the event. I was happy to oblige and deeply grateful that the event was not having the rug pulled out from under it.

As summer solstice approached about thirty people had paid in full, and another thirty had registered at sliding scale. Add to this another thirty of us working on the event plus a few guests, and it was feeling like a plentiful convocation. All of our presenters were helping to drive publicity and visibility using their personal mailing lists and social media. Stella and I offered a couple of radio and print interviews. Local astrologers we had never met shared news of the event. Chani invited Laurence Jones and Diego Fitzgerald to co-facilitate the caucuses. Tino Calenda answered my call to run our technology, and Marc Matheson nominated himself as a volunteer coordinator. The event was coming up just as big as we could handle. Over several meetings, aided by our tarot decks, we unfolded our dreams and necessary decisions into timelines and schedules.

It also happened that Linea had been left in care of Jack's astrological library. She suggested we hold a book sale, to distribute the wealth of his archives concretely into the hands of what we imagined would include many younger and perhaps greener populations. And at the same time we raised money not only to support this event, but also to create the Jack Fertig Scholarship Fund, which the SFAS administers to create access to other bay area events. The generative quality of the event was bearing even more fruit than our organizing team had envisioned.

Cancer

Two weeks before the conference a few of us walked through the quiet of the university on summer break. We confirmed the hours we were able to access the building, and made a shopping list of all that we'd want on hand for the days themselves. I made a trip to SCRAP: the Scrounger's Center for Reusable Art Parts. I found some golden star-shaped boxes to ornament the curtain backdrop in the main hall, and most of the practical supplies on the list, as well as a whole gaggle of art supplies, which we wanted for participants to use as they chose.

Further along the way, we met normal changes of plans, such as one of the video documentarians getting sick, alongside bigger shifts, such as one of the presenters needing to speak via Skype instead of travel across the country, with equal adaptive flow. Whatever was happening, the event had its own pulse and we were devoted to tending it as best as we could.

Friday before the event about thirty of us, mostly volunteers I had never met, gathered in the afternoon to load in Jack's Library, set up the two rooms we were using, and to walk though a technical schedule of the weekend. We appointed a system for a pair of people to be room monitors, responsible for tending the speakers and managing lighting and doors and such, creating tulle sashes for them in queer pastels. Chani spearheaded creating an altar space dedicated to Trayvon Martin, as Zimmerman's acquittal had been announced just days before. I was humbled by everyone's willingness to devote their Friday evening in care of our weekend together. The gift of having a venue which allowed us access a day early, in a secure space to leave our gear overnight, all at no charge, was no small miracle of the CIIS connection.

It is worth mentioning before we get to the event itself that Stella was an unwavering support at helping me stay grounded, and to articulate both my hopes for the event as well as personal goals which I hoped to achieve through my role producing it. Aware that I was imminently withdrawing from the university, I looked back at the objectives list that I had written with my application nine months prior. Nearly all of them had to do with furthering my work as an astrologer. And while it turned out that my coursework was not doing much for this, my affiliation with the institution had indeed helped all my aims become a lot more real.

Queer Astrology Conference— Saturday July 20, 2013

I picked Stella up in my car and we drove the ten minutes down Folsom street to CIIS listening to the Art Ensemble of Chicago's 'Theme do Yoyo'; She thanked me for how the tune dispersed her anxiety. This was one anchor in the playlist I had made to set the space during arrivals, this and Gary Bartz' 'Celestial Blues', a jazz gem with the lyric: Talk to the Heavenly Bodies. Sam Cooke, Herbie Hancock, Sweet Honey and other treasures filled the assembling hall. A longtime friend who came to support me posted that, seeing me dancing as I attended to details assured her the tone of the day would be celebratory. And it was.

The Opening Panel brought together all the presenters to dialogue on what had called them to the event, and to begin to articulate what Queer Astrology means to them. Whereas in other ceremonial events there would be an invocation of sacred space, this first session effected that for the weekend. Yolo arrived a little late, having flown from New York the evening before, and perhaps it was unkind for me to walk the mic over to introduce him as he had barely just arrived, and we had never met. He carried it off with great grace and dexterity, acknowledging his encounter with a dose of "West Coast Realness."

The only breakdown on Saturday was around lunch. We invited folks to opt in for Indian food delivery (eating together builds relationships) and it arrived at minute forty of our fifty minute break. In addition to me having low blood sugar and being severely cranky at the plans gone awry, I also got a shoe full of dal splashing out of the container while carrying it upstairs. To whoever cleaned the turmeric-stained mess out of the elevator, I cannot thank you enough. And to the gods, for whom every creation must contain at least some imperfection, I am grateful they exacted their toll in such an out of sight and inconsequential blip. We pushed the events back twenty minutes and the day proceeded more or less flawlessly.

Truth be told, I do not remember a lot from Saturday. I was a little fried from managing details in the lead up days and was mostly tending the edges to be sure the participant's experience was a smooth as could be. Though I was exhausted by the time the evening program began, the ritual led by Sister Barbra Ganesh was glistening. While the weekend as a whole generally looked forward toward what is yet to be done, this concrete, well-tended link to an elder/ancestor of our practice was invaluable. In many ways the whole event was resting upon Jack's spirit. And while I only knew him in passing, there were several occasions where I imagined his presence taking care of the conference.

I got a good night of sleep and made a commitment to myself to really immerse myself in the community on Sunday, trusting Saturday had gone well enough that no matter how little I was minding logistics, the conference was plenty successful already.

Queer Astrology Conference— Sunday, July 21, 2013

Chani opened the day with a brilliant welcome and huge loving appreciations for Jessica and Barry. My one regret of the weekend was that, as we a were videographer short, I somehow failed to let Kay record this talk, but rather told him since he was covering the other room that he could sit that hour out. The audio is great but the visuals were priceless.

As I was speaking later that afternoon, I opted to sit out the next round of lectures and claim a little down time. I wanted to allow myself plenty of space to actually enjoy the gathered people and the intelligences at play. During this hour Kent Bye and I caught up. He publishes interviews from astrology conferences on his Soundcloud channel: Esoteric Voices. In parallel to all the scheduled events, he conducted a full set of interviews with the presenters through the weekend.

And how did I let myself get talked into presenting a session in the midst of all this organizing?! Actually my co-conspirators insisted I take this occasion not simply to stay backstage, but to step into the formal limelight and to share and document my practice. My talk, drawing upon my mystical tendencies, was framed as a ritual. Using the chart of the day, especially the water trines, I cast a lens on what it means to relate. I shared some options for how water as an astrological element and a bodily reality may be encountered outside in the Euro-centric West, and used the watery depths of the day to suggest directing forward our relation to belonging, especially familial bonds. During a few minutes of silence at the end, I invited the room to be still within the landscape I had outlined. I myself had a uniquely mystical experience: I heard the me of the future offering unconditional support and assent for the lecture I had just given. I knew in a deep place that what had just happened in my typical extemporaneous delivery was a uniquely perfect set-up for some piece of the future of QA's work.

Both days were full of serendipity and burgeoning connections. Friendships and collegial relationship were forged and strengthened. Laughter and irreverence mixed with self-reflection and reconsideration. By the closing event the lot of us were thoroughly full. During an appreciation circle I recall Corina Dross, a new friend who came down from Portland, saying something to effect of: she had never been in a place where so many people came together sharing so many of her deepest cared-for interests. For me this summed up the event. We had called together the seeds of tribe and had successfully made a first draft at being with and in our new set of questions.

Break down and clean up was steady, and as we left the building I felt

QUEER ASTROLOGY CONFERENCE
interrupting heteronormativity one galaxy at a time
July 20 & 21, 2013   queerastrology.com

Saturday, July 20, 2013

10 – 11:40 am
Introductions & Whole Conference Panel: *"What's a Queer Astrology?"*

12 – 1:20 pm
The Compatibility Myth: Queering the Astrological Lens ~ Yolo Akili
or
Astro Drag ~ Lilia Leshan

Lunch

2:30 – 3:50 pm
Ecosexuality: Liberating the Venus within Pluto ~ Erica Jones
or
Lilith and Adam: The Origins of Gender, Sex and Deviance ~ Chani Nicholas

4:10 – 5:30 pm
The Saturn Return of AIDS ~ Christopher Renstrom
or
People of Color Caucus ~ Diego Fitzgerald
or
White Allies Caucus ~ Stella Lawson

break

7 – 9:30 pm
Tribute to Jack Fertig

Sunday, July 21, 2013

12 – 1:20 pm
Queer Talk on Client Work ~ Jessica Lanyadoo and Barry Perlman

1:40 – 3:00 pm
Queer Liberation and the Stars ~ Rod O'Neal
or
Asteroids for Beginners: Toward a Queer Feminist Astrology ~ Stella Lawson

Lunch

4:30 – 5:50 pm
Gender in Myths, Myths of Gender ~ Rhea Wolf
or
Queer Water, Queer Body, Queer Space ~ Ian Waisler

6:10 – 7:30 pm
Holistic Sexuality and Astrology ~ Eric Francis Coppolino
or
Trans / Genderqueer Caucus ~ Lucien Mae
or
Cisgender Allies Caucus ~ Chani Nicholas & Laurence Jones

7:30 pm
Closing Ritual

that we had gotten away with some sort of heist. Being profoundly out and unbridled in our inquiry felt like a provocation to the institute. Not that anything particularly racy or off color had taken place; but at the same time an event such as this had never happened before and was treading into territory whose time is now.

But beyond the not-illicit 8th house implications of a *queer* event, was the plunder; we had been gifted several thousand dollars in the form of the venue and equipment, in a way which falls outside of how the university believes itself to run. Still an event like this maximizes the potential which institutions like this promise at their best. One moral being: seek out and ask for untapped resources and let them support you as you bring your visions alive.

Afterwards, Demetrius Bagley, an organizer for several large conferences, had come out from New York. He suggested I publish some statistics on how the conference went down. This seems as good a place as any. Between sponsoring organizations, participant registrations, and in-kind donations, the conference brought in just over $7500. Actual expenses were about $5300, leaving a nest egg for ongoing work. There were 123 people on the roster when the conference began. 37 were offered full or partial scholarship. We failed to keep good record of how many walk-ins attended, but likely about 150 attended the days, while other community members came solely for Jack's memorial.

The finances of the event managed to embrace both "this is the price" and "pay what you can" ethics while still coming in ahead, with just enough money to seed our first publishing effort, but not quite enough to comfortably sponsor a next event. Fundraising continues. As of spring 2014, the audio recordings from the event were still available to the public freely, with a request that people donate toward future projects if they are able. The dance between freedom from commerce and the needs of cash is just one of the ongoing creative tensions.

As a first iteration of whatever Queer Astrology may yet be, I liken the 2013 conference to the Fool card in the tarot. The wide-open possibility of beginning full with enthusiasm remains absent past conditions. Whenever the planning hit a snag, or tied itself in a knot, I trusted there may not always a way through, but at least a step back to regain the Fool's curious willingness. From there the way continues to reveal itself.

For a next conference I have been reflecting on the next card: the Magician. The fool's self-creation remains present, but so is being more methodical around using wisdom and skill and visibility to arrive at more concrete contributions to our peers and future students. In addition to queer content offered by one or a few at the head of the room, I plan to host as many classrooms as lectures. A second gathering will aim to give shape to how Queer Astrology might self-replicate, showing up in events beyond SF and Portland. In order for this to work, those of us gathered will do well to articulate why Queer + Astrology has continued relevance.

In addition to content, I see sessions dedicated to applications of technology; perhaps we can launch a QA-wiki and co-create the textbook of our dreams.

So What?

It is possible much of what we are doing is akin to what our fellow astrologers have already done, getting curious at the intersections where traditional practices meet brand new data. It is hard to imagine another field where experts vary so widely in their expertise; this is just one way that astrology is already queered. Still, in many places on the planet such gatherings would be criminal, just as astrology has faced criminalization. And even if the same questions and even some of the same answers have been brewing among astrologers going back generations, visibility and record are some of the gifts we humbly offer to the future. Finally, where the expert/authority has historically monopolized truth, the potential in queering our astrology practices subverts hierarchy and champions listening. Just as sitting with clients evolves our book learning into something more curious than dominating, gathering as queer astrologers carries the potential to keep our practice honest—messy and honest.

There is a strength in organizing, and a healing in being together in number. In bringing focus to the unspoken terrain which us queer ones know, we claim our birthright as visionaries and healers. For QA to thrive, new and many leaders will have to take up the work. Might you hear the call?

☿

Endnotes

1 Erin D'Estrée, "Queer Astrology: Not for Queers Only," *The Mountain Astrologer*, no. 175 (June/July 2014): pp. 46–49.

2 IAD is an observance originated in 1993 by the Association for Astrological Networking as an expansion of their Astrology Awareness Weekend. The SFAS and bay area National Council for Geocosmic Research chapter have collaborated on hosting a full day of lectures, with a second-day intensive the past many years in San Francisco.

Ian Waisler is a lifelong student of astrology and other mystery schools. In addition to client work and serving as president of the San Francisco Astrological Society, he spearheaded the Queer Astrology Conference at CIIS in 2013. Look for the next one in 2015. He has been a teacher of the Integral Yoga of Swami Satchidananda since 2002. New in 2014 was team teaching Reclaiming's Elements of Magic, Rites of Passage, and Queer Pentacle. He enjoys spelunking in the gaps between received wisdom and embodied encounter, and prefers circle-shaped learning spaces over lectures delivered from the front of the room. Find his personal agenda at ianwaisler.com, and community efforts at queerastrology.com.

Reflections on a Lost Generation of Queer Astrologers
by
Gary David Lorentzen

In the spring of 2013 I was in San Francisco and attended a preliminary outreach meeting and presentation of "Queer Astrology" held at the California Institute of Integral Studies. The meeting led to the organization of the first Queer Astrology conference later that summer. It was a fascinating discussion and presentation but, although it seemed a novel idea to most everyone there, the idea was not at all new to me. I am a gay man in my sixties, have been active in the world of astrology since 1972, and, although this idea of queering astrology is only now taking hold, the conversation took me back some thirty years.

There was a significant group of gay astrologers who were very influential in the 1970s–1990s, and we had the same discussions, the same thoughts, ideas and came to the same conclusions three decades ago that I heard in this initial Queer Astrology presentation. The difference is that this new generation of astrologers who had gathered there felt liberated enough to take the discussion beyond conceptualization and make something happen. I suppose this speaks to the success and awareness of gender, feminist, and queer theory as intellectual pursuits that have developed since the 1970s and become mainstream academic interests. In itself, this is both a testament to the social changes regarding acceptance of alternative sexualities, as well as to the attitudinal changes within the astrological community regarding its own LGBT members. This new generation of astrologers is apparently well-versed in ideas like queer theory and this opens the possibility that they actually begin "queering" astrology. Our community was not so open and accepting thirty to forty years ago. There could never have been a Queer Astrology Conference in 1980 for many reasons, but, in general, minds were just not open to the idea.

So, I would like to present to you some of the ideas that we older gay astrologers had about queering astrology, but really didn't have the wherewithal to do anything about. That is, the world of astrology had not changed enough yet to embrace a queer approach to the practice, but gay astrologers were still creating among themselves a theoretical basis for what now is being called "Queer Astrology." Then I would like to introduce many of these gay men all of whom may not have been "out and proud" because they didn't feel safe, but nonetheless, they had a significant influence in changing astrology in its study, practice, application and professionalism over the last forty years.

There were a few of us who talked about gay issues just among ourselves, but we were reluctant to open up the discussion to others. I remember, whenever I tried, the reaction was always a nervous glance, hesitation, then an immediate change of subject. So, it was something that we talked about quietly together at conferences or, in my case, with my friend, Bruce Hamerslough—one of the first astrologers to just matter-of-factly come out and even say he was HIV positive—we sat down and decided to prioritize issues we wanted to know more about. Our clientele in Seattle was increasingly gay, and neither of us felt that we had any meaningful way of approaching an astrological counseling session with them without coming out to them ourselves in order to make them feel more comfortable. But we were concerned that doing so would make the session more about us than about them, so there had to be another way. We began to realize that there was something wrong with the astrology, or at least with the approach and interpretations in which we had been schooled. It was a little disconcerting to think that we had no theory or interpretive framework for dealing even with ourselves much less with gay clients.

One of the first issues I remember studying with Bruce was the idea of a "gay signature" in the birth chart. Based on the literature, there were many different "signatures" suggested by the astrologers of the day and those from earlier in the century, all of which reflected the misinformed opinion that there was something pathological with homosexuality. For example, there was the commonly held belief that "hard" aspects between Venus and Saturn in a man's chart made it difficult for him to relate to women, so his sexuality would constellate around an erotic attraction to a father figure. The same sort of "interpretations" was given to "hard" Moon/Saturn aspects. Another was any "hard" Mars/Venus/Uranus aspect pattern perverted the sexual impulse and redirected the "natural attraction" away from women and towards men. Lesbians suffered from Mars/Neptune "afflictions"—they were simply confused and sought sisterly affection from their female friends, but with the right man, all would be well. You see the problem immediately looking at it from today's experience and perspective! Somehow, it often escaped astrologers that even heterosexuals have such aspects in their charts and they weren't considered as signatures for heterosexuality. I often heard these offensive interpretations at conference presentations and read them in articles as well as in sections of books. Yet, in spite of the fact the American Psychiatric Association had de-pathologized homosexuality in 1973, attitudes and interpretations were very slow to change in the astrological community.

Even within my Boomer generation of astrologers, many of whom were influenced by Jung and archetypal approaches stemming from Joseph Campbell's work in mythology, there was difficulty in reconciling concepts like "syzygy" (reconciliation of opposites, i.e., male and female archetypes in the psyche) and its manifestation in male-female sexual attraction, and the realities of same-sex attraction. The late Tony Joseph and I had conversations about this problem and even he, as an archetypal astrologer and gay man, could not comfortably conform Jungian theory to a homosexual orientation. But then, within Jungian circles, there was also controversy over how to explain homosexuality within the limits of Jungian theory. If depth psychology was going to be used for astrological work, then theories like analytical psychology had to be applied. At least that was the conventional wisdom. Freud's idea of a universal "latent homosexuality" was being discredited in academia, so for astrology the Jungian archetypal approach seemed a better fit, but it didn't provide any real answers either.

Thus, chart interpretations were (and often still are) hetero-centrically biased and ignorant in their assumptions about sexuality. It is no wonder that astrologers didn't feel comfortable openly discussing queer and gay issues. There was no theoretical basis within the literature or schools of thought for doing so. Astrologers all too often, like psychologists prior to the 1970s, conflated the effects of society on the emotional lives of gay people with their sexuality. That is to say, the depression, anxiety, emotional stress and self-loathing that actually come from being closeted in an intensely homophobic society, were rather seen as a result of a pathological sexuality, and not seen as stemming from the oppression of living in a frighteningly hateful world. Some of that ignorance is still around because astrology is too often a self-study and the old materials and books with questionable interpretations and assumptions are still available and being used.

Obviously, at this point in time, it is pretty well established that there is no astrological signature for homosexuality. Sexuality is now seen more as an identity and orientation to the world based on a multiplicity of factors from genetics to very early responses to the environment, not unlike culture, nationality or gender, none of which can be "found" in the planetary placements

Samuel Araya's "Rusalka – Pisces," for the Constellation *art show*

Constructed around the mutability of the sign, this piece was conceived with a mixture of photography and painting—photography being a vehicle of memory and painting a tool for communication with the dreamworld, in the threshold between these two worlds. It is not the first iteration, as it has lived five times before in several guises. The work was constructed with water-based media (watercolors, gouache), paints that come back to life with a splash of water; so once a "finished" stage was reached, it was subsequently destroyed, layers and detritus remaining to serve as the foundation of the next "final" painting, only to be wiped out, again and again. The perpetual movement arrived finally to Rusalka, the water nymph of Slavic legend, quoting Kafka:

"Now the Sirens have a still more fatal weapon than their song, namely their silence...someone might possibly have escaped from their singing; but from their silence, certainly never."

of the birth chart. There are probably as many different "signatures" for sexuality as there are people, and this fact requires us all to be acutely sensitive to our clients' individual sexual orientations and gender identities.

Yet, gay people who go to astrologers often experience the same old prejudices that I experienced in astrology forty years ago. In general, we still too often see the Uranus/Neptune/Pluto/Venus/Mars combinations as potential indicators of homosexuality, rather than seeing the client simply as a sexual being, whether gay, straight, bi, or transgendered, and interpreting the planetary dynamics as to how they come to know and deal with their sexuality. But this is exactly what gay astrologers were formulating back in the early 1980s and what today's younger astrologers, whatever their sexuality, are trying to do today with their "Queer Astrology." There needs to be a body of work on the subject that becomes the basis for a new, less hetero-centric approach, in order to make this somewhat separate queer branch of interpretation more accepted and generalized in common practice.

There is an important, oft forgotten reason for the lack of a body of queer astrological work from the 1970s through the 1990s. Aside from the historical, theoretical and interpretive problems in astrology regarding sexuality, dealing with gay clients and acknowledging gay practitioners, there was also the added terror of the AIDS epidemic that began in the early 1980s and made the situation much worse for gay astrologers. Although I would like to believe that my astro-colleagues were, for the most part, less paranoid of their gay counterparts than, say the general population was, it was still problematic. People mentioned "gay" only in side conversations and whispers, which made many of us very uncomfortable. But then our colleagues started dying of AIDS, and it simply couldn't be ignored anymore. Some of us began to realize staying quiet (i.e. closeted) was not a good idea. My friend, Bruce, and I had long heart-to-heart conversations about coming out, making the astrological community more aware, and imploring them to be more compassionate as we began losing many of our best and brightest astrologers.

I first met Bruce Hamerslough in Atlanta in 1978. Originally, from New York, he was living in Athens, and I had just moved to Atlanta. I immediately joined the Metro Atlanta Astrological Society, for which Bruce then was the Vice President, and we started a congenial professional relationship. I moved back to Seattle in late 1979 and Bruce moved there in the early 1980s. We became good friends, and I spent a lot of time with him and his business partner and fellow astrologer, Dennis Flaherty, before Bruce died. Bruce believed he had been HIV positive probably since 1980 or '81, so the subject was emotionally close to him. He and I discussed at length the issue of HIV and sexuality in astrological interpretation, and we wanted to have open discussions about the AIDS crisis with others, but it wasn't at all a welcome conversation. We realized then it felt too risky to promote such a thing in the community-at-large, because there was so much fear and confusion around the subject. As a result, our notion of "queer astrology," that is, making the community open and welcoming to gay practitioners, dealing appropriately with gay and lesbian clients, and publishing articles and perhaps even books, never went anywhere except as an interesting topic of conversation among ourselves and a few other gay astrologers. The very idea of researching and creating a body of work around the issues of homosexuality was becoming less and less likely.

During the 1980s, because of the slow response to the crisis, gay people all over the world started getting angry and holding massive protests regarding gay rights and AIDS. Governments simply dismissed the diseased initially as a "gay disease" and there was not much of a concerted effort to deal with it. It took a great deal of "acting up and out" to get their attention. Finally, there was an appropriate response to the epidemic, but the delay meant the death of millions. Within the astrological community, men started dying of AIDS and AIDS related problems, which Bruce and I thought required some kind of response from astrologers. At least, the gay astrologers needed to stand up and make it known. Bruce and I decided we would not stay closeted, but we were both a bit shy about it because we were concerned about our reputations in the community. We didn't make any dramatic announcements, but starting in 1986, we simply let it be known through normal communication with others that we were gay. Of course, no one seemed to care. Yet, at the national level, many of our best astrologers, who also happened to be gay, were not coming out, and they were dying. It was a terrible situation, yet no one was talking about it or dealing with it.

It turned into a tragic period in the history of modern astrology, because we lost many brilliant young astrologers to the AIDS epidemic in the late 1980s and 1990s, including my friend, Bruce. It was a devastating blow to the global astrological community, and many of us lost close friends and teachers, not to mention the loss of continued research, writing and general contributions to the discipline and profession, and most specifically in the area of sexuality and queer theory. I think it is time to remind ourselves not only who these men were and that they were very important to the global community, but also of what we were trying to accomplish in the field of astrology. Since the movement for a Queer Astrology is gaining momentum again, I would like to introduce these gay men to remember and examine what came before the current movement, to be inspired by their work, and, if nothing else, just to appreciate them.

Here is a list of American astrologers who paved the way for what is happening today in astrology, and who ultimately died of AIDS related illness or complications: *Robert Cole, Frederick Davies, Jack Fertig, Bruce Hamerslough, Jesse Portis Helm, Richard Idemon, Tony Joseph, Richard Lovell, Buz Myers, Marc Robertson, Howard Sasportas, James Farrell, Stephen Wirmusky, and Johnny Lister*. I don't know how complete this list is. These are the names that I am aware of, and I certainly hope there aren't more. If you did not know or were not aware of these men, then perhaps it is time to become acquainted at least with their names. To that end, here is a short biography and commentary, as much as I could find or remember, for many of those listed above. Where it was possible, I included the birth and death data. I wish I had known all of them, but for those I knew or with whom I was acquainted, I offer my impressions and memories.

¶ ROBERT COLE (May 7, 1948, 5:18AM PDT in Henderson, NV) was an astrologer from the Bay Area who was best known for his book, *The Book of Houses*. He was a bit of a controversial figure who often poked at the flimsy professionalism of some astrologers and whose letters to the astrological publications were often confrontational and provocative. But he made us think and reflect on what we were doing and what we were saying to our clients. He played the role of our conscience in many ways, and helped us with our integrity. He died of AIDS on August 13, 1992.

¶ JESSE PORTIS HELM (August 31, 1947, 10:35AM EDT in Brooklyn, NY) was a working astrologer who was known for his acute observations and solid, common-sense advice. As a result, he had a large practice and lectured and taught in Manhattan most of his life. Later, he moved to the Raleigh-Durham area and toward the end of his life he went to Miami. He was also a gifted Tarot reader and a student of the Kabbalah. He never really promoted himself much on the national stage, preferring instead always to focus on the people in his locality, many of whom were LGBT. It is assumed he shied away from the national scene because he was very "out" in New York and the national astrological community was not perceived as very gay friendly at the time. His writing career included a culture and entertainment column for *Gentlemen's Quarterly*, and although he never published an astrological book, his writings for his classes, lectures and workshops were legendary. His lasting legacy in astrology is the human face he brought to the discipline with his openness and compassion for his clients and students and probably some of the best teaching and self-generated astrological materials of his day. Jesse died in Miami in June of 1989 and was preceded in death by his husband of many years, Phillip Weathers, who also died of AIDS.

¶ RICHARD LOVELL (no birth data available) was also from Brooklyn, NY, and was known for his sardonic wit and one-liners about the male and female stereotypes of each sign. Richard is probably one of the least known astrologers of the era, but he used to go to every possible conference and often rattled our cages with his irreverence and his obvious attempts to deflate egos, yet he never made people uncomfortable with his humorous attacks on self-importance. He became ill with AIDS fairly early on and spent nearly a decade struggling with his health, which took him away from his astrological practice and the lecture circuit. He died in 1993.

¶ HOWARD SASPORTAS (April 12, 1948, 1:46AM EST in Hartford, CT) was one of the most influential astrologers of his day. He received his MA in Humanistic Psychology from Antioch University-NYC and in 1973 moved to London to study astrology at the Faculty of Astrological Studies. He received his FAS Gold Medal in 1979 and began teaching for them. He also studied for a degree in Psychosynthesis and in 1983, together with Liz Greene, founded the Centre for Psychological Astrology in London. He had a reputation for being a very kind, approachable professional who touched many people's lives and for his body of work that integrated psychology and astrology so well. Howard died on May 12, 1992 at 05:12PM in London, England. Here is a list of his published works: *The Twelve Houses; The Gods of Change; The Inner Planets; The Development of the Personality; Dynamics of the Unconscious.*

¶ TONY JOSEPH (December 7, 1946, 12:35AM in Cleveland, OH) was also a hugely popular and influential astrologer of the 1970s and early 1980s. He was especially known for his vast knowledge of mythology and its relationship to astrology, and together with Eleanor Bach and Demetra George, probably the most knowledgeable about asteroids. He was one of the first "archetypal" astrologers who were intellectually influenced by Joseph Campbell and C.G. Jung. Tony was charming, handsome, collegiate and very articulate. His lectures were always inspiring and his ability to connect with people whom he met for the first time was amazing. He often wanted to let people know that he was gay, but he would do so with a touch of humor and euphemism. For example, when I first met him, he asked me grinning slyly and with a sparkle in his eye, whether I was also "puer eternis" (Latin for "eternal youth"), which made me laugh. We became good professional acquaintances at that point, and he stayed with me when he came to Seattle for presentations, lectures, and workshops. Tony became the Director of the National Council for Geocosmic Research in 1979 and was active in the organization of astrology along new intellectual lines until his death. He died on June 6, 1986 at 3PM in San Francisco.

¶ STEVEN WIMURSKY (June 27, 1956, no time available) was a New York astrologer who had a passion for the theater. His professional life encompassed both astrology and the theater, and he was enthusiastic about both. Steven took astrology and his practice seriously, and he wanted to see the field become more professional and more legitimate. He always sought to improve his knowledge and his skills both with techniques as well as with his clients. He studied for and passed his professional certification from NCGR-Professional Astrologers' Alliance. He had a significant astrological practice which included consciously and purposefully serving the gay community, but he was also the Director of Operations for the Circle in the Square Theater. Many older astrologers might remember him from the UAC conference in Washington DC in 1992 when he was the stage manager for Michael Lutin's "Alien Follies." Steven began exhibiting HIV related symptoms shortly thereafter, and he died November 22, 1993 in Brewster MA.

¶ BRUCE HAMERSLOUGH (October 26, 1948, 06:45PM in New York, NY) grew up in Scarsdale NY, studied biology and education in college, and did his student teaching and became a public school science teacher in Vermont. But he had a passion for astrology and abandoned his teaching profession to become an astrologer. He moved to Athens, GA where he opened a metaphysical bookstore and practiced his astrology. He was instrumental in the early days of the astrological association in Atlanta, serving both as Vice President and President of that organization. He studied for and received his professional astrological certification in 1983 and moved to Seattle. There he formed a business partnership with Dennis Flaherty, and they opened the Greenlake Metaphysical Center.

Bruce was one of the first openly gay astrologers to come out as both gay and HIV positive. He had a successful practice in Seattle and he often expressed concern about gay and "queer" issues in astrology, especially when it came to serving his gay clientele. Bruce was known for his sense of humor and ability to laugh at himself as he became more ill. He developed pneumonia in late 1995, and realizing his body couldn't fight off the disease, he refused further treatment so as not to prolong the inevitable. Before he died, he asked to have this as his epitaph: "Having a wonderful time! Wish you were here!" He often said that you can lose your health, but you should never lose your sense of humor. He lived that philosophy to the end. He died December 27, 1995 at about 07:30AM in Seattle. Bruce published two books, *Forecasting Backwards and Forwards* and *The I-Ching Manual*.

¶ ROBERT "BUZ" MEYERS (November 9, 1941, 06:48PM in Painesville, OH) was another incredibly influential and popular astrologer the 1970s–1990s. He had a passion for Native American philosophy and spirituality and often infused those perspectives into his work. He was a standard fixture at all the conferences both national and international, had a very popular tape series, and wrote books that had such a unique perspective on astrology and its applications that it was hard not to read his material from cover to cover in one sitting. He was known for his sharp insights, wit, and brilliant ideas. He was dynamic and charismatic in public, yet a quiet, shy man in private and often preferred the limelight shine elsewhere. Buz was one of the few astrologers who did a great deal of work in sexuality, sexual identity and orientation. His groundbreaking lecture series and resulting book, simply titled, *Sexuality*, turned out to be one of the first attempts to "queer" astrology and move beyond stereotypes and pathological descriptions, although Buz would probably not have labeled his work "queer" at the time. Other publications include *Getting On-Time with Your Life* and *The Moon as Trigger for Transformation*. Buz died March 12, 2000 at 08:38PM in Portsmouth, VA.

¶ MARC ROBERTSON (February 8, 1937, 05:48AM PST in Mount Vernon, WA) I am including Marc here, although his "reported" cause of death was heart failure. I knew him personally; he and his colleague, Joanne Wickenburg, were my teachers at the old Astrology Center of the Northwest. He probably had more influence on my understanding and application of astrology than any other astrologer at the time. He was a very quiet, withdrawn, shy man who was a brilliant astrologer and, in spite of his reserved nature, could give a terrific public lecture. He could also be a bit of a tyrant and a diva to those around him. His body of written work, however, is incomparable and his contribution to astrology with his "cosmopsychology" can't be underestimated.

He had a fascination with human sexuality and he and I had a couple of in-depth conversations about the subject, in which he hinted at his sexual orientation, but never said he was gay. But then he never revealed anything about his personal life to anyone, ever, not even inconsequential little details that people normally discuss with others in general conversation. His book, *Using the Birth Chart to Determine Sex, Mind and Habit,* is a significant early contribution to Queer Astrology, but Marc's social conditioning and closeted nature are still evident even in his attempt to move beyond such personal limitations. Other important works include *Transit of Saturn; Engine of Destiny: Planets and Personality; Not a Sign in the Sky but a Living Person; Time out of Mind: The Past in your Astrological Birth Chart and Reincarnation; Eith House: Sex, Death and Money*. Marc Robertson died September 26, 1984.

¶ RICHARD IDEMON (There are no birth data available for Richard because he never revealed his birthday, and even those who know still respect his wish that no one knows his birthday and time.) Richard was the charismatic astrological educator par

"Ovum Saturnas," by Tobi Nussbaum, for the Constellation *art show*

excellence during the 1980s. He was famous internationally for his incredible lectures, depth of research and, probably most significantly, for his work in depth psychology together with Liz Greene. He was also the teacher for many of our most successful astrologers today. He had a tape series which was very popular both in the States and in Europe. He never wrote a full astrological book while he was still alive, but thanks to the work of Gena Ceaglio and the late Howard Sasportas, two books were published posthumously based on transcriptions of Richard's lectures, workshops and other written work: *The Magic Thread* and *Through the Looking Glass*. Richard was one of the most popular and influential astrologers and teachers of the 1980s. He died in San Francisco around noon on February 22, 1987.

These astrologers left a remarkable legacy and their deaths were hard to comprehend or accept. They were our colleagues, friends, teachers, mentors, and heroes, but their memories live on, their works are still here to be read and studied, and their influence will reach far into the future. Collectively, they formed the basis for what we are now calling Queer Astrology and the door is now open for the next generation of astrologers to complete the work and fulfill the promise of an astrology stripped of its narrow stereotypes, judgments, prejudices and misinformation about human sexuality and relationships.

☿

Acknowledgement and thanks go to Erin Sullivan, Donna Cunningham and Alan Oken for their insights and input in helping me remember and reminding me of some of the details about these men and events over the last forty years.

Gary Lorentzen has been active in the field of astrology since 1972. He has been president of both the Washington State and Oregon Astrological Associations and was a founding board member for Kepler College, responsible for the development of the curriculum and instructional designs and negotiating with the state for the approval of the B.A. in Astrological Studies. He is currently collaborating with Tony Dickey integrating astro periods of history with Tony's Planetary Wave Theory.

Astrological Remediation:
An Introduction *to* Theory and Methodology
by Andrea L. Gehrz

Have you ever found yourself looking at an astrological chart, only to observe a challenging planetary placement looking back at you? Perhaps you have been asked to look into the chart of a friend's newborn baby, and you notice a potentially intense set of energies that could cause hardship later in life. What could we tell our friend in this case? These are just a few examples of the challenging scenarios that face any practicing astrologer.

After working as a professional astrologer for over ten years, there came a point at which I could no longer stand idly by, observing the malaise and joy brought with the ebb and flow of the planets. Having watched these waves move through my own life, as well as the lives of my friends and clients, I had often felt like a helpless observer. I craved some sort of method to heal and help challenging natal charts, as well as during times of great planetary duress. I wanted to help people channel energies into their highest possible manifestations. Soon after my daughter was born, I was compelled to focus my study of astrology entirely onto methods of astrological remediation. I began to think hard on ways to aid people in moving through difficult and potent time periods. I came to understand that, whatever the nature of the time period, there is always something that can be done to make life a little bit easier or more productive.

It is my goal in this article to provide an introduction to the craft of providing remedies for astrological charts. First, we will begin with an introduction to the term itself; *astrological remediation*. We will then look into the philosophy behind remediation, as well as some ethical considerations. Next we will delve into various ways to enhance and move vibrations, followed by a short survey of methods that any astrologer can use to remedy challenges found in the natal chart.

Introduction to Astrological Remediation

As we attempt to set out a beginning into the art of *astrological remediation,* it will be necessary to clarify some basic operational definitions.

First, we must ask the simple question—what is astrology? Astrology could be defined as, "the study of how the heavenly bodies affect emotional, mental, and physical life on earth." One unifying characteristic found in all branches of astrology is the use of planetary positions to analyze aspects of earthly existence. The exactitude and nature of the information gleaned from the chart will however depend upon a number of factors. The mental, emotional, and philosophical framework of the astrologer reading the chart is one of the most important considerations. The information conveyed will also depend on what is currently happening within the systems indicated by that chart.

The process of two astrologers examining an astrological chart could be likened to two auto mechanics reading the same electrical diagram for a car. The layout of electrical circuitry for the car would be exactly the same. The manner in which each mechanic uses this information will vary, depending upon the symptoms presenting in the car, as well as the ways in which the mechanic has been trained to troubleshoot and solve problems. The astrological chart can easily be thought of as a schematic diagram of the celestial bodies. As astrologers, we examine *astral schematics* in order to observe changes in planetary movements. We then observe how these planetary movements affect human emotions, behaviors, physical health, etc.

Next, let us look into the *natal chart*. The natal chart can be thought of as a map of the planetary positions at the moment of a birth. The natal chart functions as a schematic diagram through which a passionate and dedicated astrologer can understand the intricacies of a person's "heavenly body," in order to attend to the needs of that individual soul. The natal chart can be used to inquire about a person's vibration, the state and tendencies of that person's astral and physical body, and the areas of life into which the soul will be pulled. We could propose that each person has a vibrational pattern which is locked within the DNA, cells, soul, and heart. This vibrational pattern is indicated by the astrological chart for the moment of birth.

What then is astrological remediation? *Astrological remediation* could be described as "the use of any method necessary to heal and soothe challenges that appear within the chart." This can include problematic planets or aspects that have existed from birth, or those that have come in through the moving vibrations of the traveling planets. A unique characteristic of astrological remediation is that it inherently examines and accepts the vibrational foundation of the individual who is seeking help. If astrology could be described as a detailed study of individuality, then astrological remediation could be understood as a fascinating journey into highly individualized healing methods.

Remediation has been common throughout the ancient astrological traditions, yet seems to have become a sparse topic in the modern, Western thought structure. In the Eastern traditions, remediation has been consistently used and developed throughout the centuries. A traditional Indian astrologer might prescribe the use of certain gems to remedy problems within the chart, or prescribe a mantra to her client in order to mitigate the harsh qualities of a certain period of time. A spiritual pilgrimage to a sacred site may also be prescribed for a problem deep within the soul. In medieval times, astrological remediation was often practiced through the use of talismans, amulets, alchemy, and spells.

In her timeless book *Hands of Light*, Barbara Brennan expertly describes the energy-body and the existence of illness as beginning within the vibrational field. The "light body" or aura is very much connected with the soul. Astrology provides a language through which we can explain and describe the needs and tendencies of a particular soul, as well as the details of that person's "solar apparatus."

Astrological remediation is an extremely useful method of healing because it inherently approaches each situation as unique, attempting to understand and fix the etheric roots of the problem at hand. The methods through which an astrological remedialist will help or heal will depend upon the skills of each practitioner. The common goal among remedialists is to manage temperamental intensities that may be causing unwanted problems or behaviors, so that troubling expressions can be allowed to change or perhaps even fade away.

Astrological remediation could most simply be defined as:

The use of astrology to heal people, make life more enjoyable, and release suffering.

People often ask me why I choose to use the word *"remediation."* The answer for this is simple. The word *remediation* suggests an ongoing process of providing remedies. If we are to assume that the traveling planets continue to affect us and alter our energetic field throughout the span of life, then we can attempt to provide remedies throughout this entire evolutionary process. From this perspective, our work as remedialists is never done, as we make it our goal to provide necessary aid through life's myriad of changes and challenges.

A Look into Ethical Considerations:

Whether or not we understand it, as practitioners of astrology, we hold a sacred responsibility to uphold good thoughts in the minds of our clients. When we have a client's "life map" in front of us, we are being entrusted with the power to help them understand who they are, who they have been thus far, and who they can be in the future. In fact, as is true with any consultant's practice, we also must be careful to avoid ethical problems such as conflicts of interest, dual relationship issues, etc. We will also be wise to acknowledge the power differential that exists between the astrological remedialist and the client. Ethical considerations could be a topic for an entire article, yet we will attempt to cover a little ground here. The first ethical lesson in the art of astrological remediation is to:

DO NO HARM

At a most basic level, we want to make sure that we are not incidentally causing strife in the lives of our clients. To begin thinking on the importance of such concerns, any serious remedialist would be wise to get acquainted with the code of ethics laid out by the Organization of Professional Astrologers. The OPA addresses the issue thoroughly, suggesting that:

Every astrologer take full responsibility for the information he or she is imparting, and that every client be treated in a thoughtful, sensitive manner. This includes refraining from making statements that may be stressful to the client and that may not be true, such as predicting someone will never marry, never have children, or die at a specific time.

In the most simple sense, we do not want to suggest that our clients are destined for horrible futures. In fact, it might be said that the only good reason to look into the future is to help create a brighter one. Not only can we foster healthy client-consultant relationships by doing certain acts, we can also take a few practical precautions to avoid incidentally contributing to a harsh future. Here are just a few ideas:

Let us:

Describe our role as remedialists clearly to clients.
Accept jobs only of which we are qualified.
Ask for appropriate & clear compensation.
Maintain client privacy.

Let us not:

Suggest that horrible things might happen.
Look aghast at something in the chart.
Assign negative labels to parts of the chart.
Give the client no choices about their future.
Describe hard energies without framing the information in a useful manner.

These are just a few thoughts on the ethics of "doing no harm." As the field of astral healing continues to grow, a formal code of ethics will surely be written. Until that time comes, we as remedialists can continue to uphold a high ethical standard within our own work. There does not exist a school for astrological remediation, yet we can be creative in the ways in which we continue to learn. Developing and practicing our own methods will advance the field organically. We can even extract wisdom from ethical codes in other disciplines, helping us to learn even more about how to avoid incidentally harming our clients.

On Radical Free Will:

When engaging in the art of astrological remediation, it is important to always keep *free will* in mind. The subject of "fate vs. free will" has been a passionate and frequent topic of debate within the astrological community. *Free will* can most simply be defined as: *The freedom to exert one's will.* In relation to astrology, free will could be thought of as: *The freedom to be in charge of one's own planetary energies, existence, destiny, future, karma, and life experiences.*

While we as astrologers might never know the true answer to the fate vs. free will debate, it is probably true that each life is allowed a little of both. In other words, our lives are probably a combination of certain fated occurrences that can coexist with a certain amount of freedom to choose. For instance, there are fated relationships in each of our lives; immediate relatives, some of our lovers, the boss at the job we've had for five years, etc. There is also a certain fatedness in the wiring of our personal temperament, as is indicated by our astrological chart. With this understanding in mind, we can easily accept that there will be energies and karma acting upon and within us as we move into our futures.

That being said, as practicing astrologers, it is necessary to develop language about the concepts of fate and free will. Our clients often need some extra encouragement towards their own free will, especially after witnessing the accuracy of astrology's past predictions. Astrology's uncanny precision can leave a client feeling shocked at the seeming fatedness of everything. Each astrologer must of course discover his or her own beliefs in this area. It is my particular belief and experience that when used correctly, astrology can be one of the most healing studies in existence, but in order to truly heal, we must use a *radical free will* approach as we engage in astrological analysis.

The *radical free will* philosophy can be likened to certain martial arts that work with the energies of one's opponent. The teachers of these disciplines instruct the martial artist in the skill of harnessing his opponent's chi, using this energy for the fighter's own protection. For instance, such a fighter would be able to use the forward motion of a charging opponent to flip the enemy onto his back. Within the *radical free will* approach to astrology, the planetary energies are to be worked with, harnessed, used, floated upon, wrangled, and even enjoyed. At times, and always with the consent of all parties involved, the planetary energies are also to be deflected, manipulated, and altered.

A philosophy such as this allows the client to make choices about how they will use challenging and pleasant vibrations, both now and in the future. When taking on a free will oriented approach, all things are malleable. If we assume that astrology is in fact successful at predicting certain feelings, events, or energies in the life, and we also accept that these energies are to be managed, handled, and even dissipated through certain remedial measures, then we will have arrived at a very effective and helpful way to use astrology.

In terms of philosophy, I would also like to stress the importance of each astrological remedialist working from the stance of their own higher worldview. This is important when dealing with matters of the soul and spirit, as life can at times be altogether challenging. Some remedialists may have a background in Buddhist philosophy, while others may be soothed by a more cerebral stance such as Act Utilitarianism, a philosophy that makes decisions for the greatest of all concerned.

What philosophical framework do you use to make decisions during hard moments, transits, consultations, etc.?

GOALS OF ASTROLOGICAL REMEDIATION:

While there are many goals to remediation, it will be useful to look at a few aims here.

GOAL ONE: OPEN THE HEART TO ITS HIGHEST PURPOSE

The astrological chart can be seen as a map of personal temperament. It might be said that each temperament has a certain cultural value. Earthy types, for instance, could be said to provide an industrious and structuring gift to the world, while watery persons may be wired towards the more emotional aspects of life. By keeping in mind and speaking to the highest possibilities in any chart, we can best allow our clients the opportunity to express their positive potentials.

GOAL TWO: OPTIMIZE THE PHYSICAL CONSTITUTION

Because an astrological chart is representative of our "photonic make-up," it also shows the parts of our physical structure that are sturdy and buoyant, as well as those that may tend to become compromised. It is helpful to let our clients in on their elemental make-up, as different constitutions are balanced and healed in different ways. For instance, if a person is found to be prone to ear infections and we find that they have natal Mars in Taurus, we can try to mitigate the heat coming into the system a few different ways. We can cool it down with ice packs, change the environment in the ear with a few drops of Apple Cider Vinegar, or use some cooling herbs.

Practices such as *symbolic substitution* can harness and redirect energies within the body, in order to prevent vibrations from building up in the physical form. In this case, we might want to try an expulsion of heat through an act such as power-lifting, building a stone wall, or feverishly collecting and counting money. All of these activities could be considered ways to redirect the energies of Mars, and could potentially move the ionized heat of Mars through the earthly body system of Taurus.

There are many methods through which to improve our physical constitution by looking at the astrological chart. It would be beneficial for any astrological remedialist to learn a bit about astrophysiognomy, medical astrology, and esoteric anatomy.

Goal Three: Enhance the communicative process & personal narrative

Because our mental state affects how we interface with the world, it is important to maintain a healthy, happy narrative about one's life. Our narrative could be described as the words, language, and stories we construct about our personal experience. At a most basic level, the non-judgmental lens of the astrology can help to provide a positive, spiritual framework for any life circumstance. We can do this by speaking to the highest potential in the charts of our clients and giving supporting, productive language to difficult time periods. As astrologers, we have the blessed opportunity to provide a positive framework about even the most challenging of struggles!

Vibrational Enhancements:

When we come across a challenging planet, angle, or transit, one of our jobs as remedialists will be to attempt to soften harsh energies. There are countless ways to move and morph energy. Here are a few examples.

- *Transfer:* To move an energy or vibration.
- *Deflection:* To stop an energy from entering the system.
- *Balancing:* To bring a new energy in to balance the existing state.
- *Attraction:* To encourage new energies to enter the field.
- *Enhancement:* To add to the already existing vibrations.
- *Neutralization:* To render an energy neutral through an opposing force.
- *Morphing:* To alter or change a vibrational state.

Methodologies:

Countless methods can be used to transfer, deflect, balance, and attract energies. The special techniques used by each astrological remedialist can be tailored to that person's natural gifts and skill sets. Some remedialists come into the field of astrology with an expertise in herbalism. Such practitioners might attempt to balance hard natal and transiting angles through the use of herbs. For instance, an herbalist might counteract Martian vibrations with a Venusian remedy, or some cooling herbs.

If a remedialist were also an expert in music, she might attempt to neutralize a harsh energy through the use of musical vibrations. For instance, if a client is in a Pluto/Mars transit, the

> *What kinds of remedies do you naturally prefer to use for what ails you, your family, friends, etc.? In what ways could you combine these methods with astrology?*

musical remedialist might recommend listening to some driving goth-industrial music to match the intensity of the resonance. This could help to neutralize the negativity of the highly intensified state. One way of morphing energies through music would be to play uplifting music during a Saturnian moment. Such music could alter the depressed resonance of Saturn. Music can also be used to transfer the energies of the planets through the physical body, especially if we engage in the act of playing music ourselves.

As is becoming clear, each astrological remedialist will have their own specialties.

Now, let us look into a few useful techniques to get any astrologer equipped to begin optimizing the life experience through astrology: strategic planning, symbolic substitution, astral merging/intentional compositing, astro-cartography, and gem remedies.

Strategic Planning

Once we have watched a chart in real time through a study of the transits, it is easier to know how a person ticks. Some charts are very hard working at times, and then tend to relax heavily. Other people meander throughout life, not flaring up much at all. A person with most of their planets in one sign will be quite focused in their activities. A chart with planets scattered throughout may manifest into a life that is more haphazard.

By becoming aware of the patterns in a chart, we can then attempt to work with the natural influx of planetary energies. If the upcoming year will be heavily influenced by Saturn, we will want to prepare for hard work, and to be schooled in some fashion. If Jupiter will be prominent, we will have the natural urge to expand, and thus it might be a year ripe for growth. Martian periods are good for differentiation, while Venusian periods are more apt for connection. For persons who have intense chart configurations, strategic planning can be quit helpful in maximizing the life experience.

- *Strategic Planning through the use of the planets can be as simple as:*
- *Setting deadlines for the ending of certain transits.*
- *Planning important public appearances on Venus/Sun days.*
- *Planning to constrict the finances under Saturn transits.*
- *Planning to go to networking meetings while under the influence of Jupiter.*
- *Doing activities that require gusto on Mars transits.*
- *Seeking love on transits involving Venus.*

Symbolic Substitution

Symbolic substitution allows energetic neutralization, deflection, transfer, absorption, etc., to occur through worldly activities that naturally satisfy the soul's needs. Certain unchanneled longings might cause unwanted behaviors or physical symptoms. In symbolic substitution, we use a very simple, two-step process. The first part of the process will be to locate an energetic cluster in the astrological chart which is causing unwanted patterns. The second step is to find activities and outlets into which the problem-causing tendencies can most gloriously be channeled. By finding apt places to pour abundant energies or honor constrictions, we create a veritable landscape upon which to become more centered, productive, happy versions of ourselves.

The basic premise behind symbolic substitution is the substitution of hard planetary energies with easier or more fruitful expressions of the vibes. We might best approach this topic with a metaphor. Suppose there is a river that is gushing strongly into the foundation of our house. This will of course deteriorate the structure under which we live. Symbolic substitution would be the act of re-routing this river so that its inherent power can do some good work in our life. While it might require a bit of effort and time to re-route the river, the benefit in the end will be obvious.

Each planet symbolizes a certain facet of life. There are many ways to handle, wrangle, and use the quality of each planet. Suppose a child keeps getting overheated, which leads to behavioral outbursts. Now suppose that we discover the problematic planet to be an extremely hot Mars. While certain remedial techniques will focus on cooling off or neutralizing the overheated Mars, symbolic substitution would work to provide an alternate outlet for the heated nature. We can often find great success in channeling the heat through introducing a new activity into the life. In the example of the overheated child, we could begin by asking ourselves any of the following questions:

¶ *What would be a non-problematic use of the ultra-hot energy of Mars?*
¶ *What body system is getting heated up?*
¶ *Is there an activity that would allow the energy of Mars to be expressed without hurting anyone?*
¶ *Is there a use of Mars that would not be disgraceful or frustrating?*

Astral Merging and Intentional Compositing

It is possible to minimize time spent hanging around people with whom we meld poorly. In fact, one way to maximize happiness is by engaging heartily in beneficial and uplifting relationships. By allowing other vibrations to mix with our own we can neutralize, absorb, or even enhance certain parts of ourselves. It could be suggested that this is how the use of certain stones or metals can work to neutralize our vibrational fields. Keeping these objects on our person will surely change the tone, color, and quality of our energetic fluxings. This process also occurs when we commune with another person, animal, town, etc. By bringing new energies into and around ourselves, we inherently alter our own life sphere. This is one of the most fun ways to remedy hard parts of our charts! By spending time with people we love, who validate and heal the hardest parts of ourselves, we can ensure brighter futures. We can also alter our lives by moving to a new town; one which has different qualities from the one in which we have been feeling stagnant. New vibes can even enter our fields through a short trip.

In terms of using "astral merging" as remediation, we will want to focus on the technique of *intentional compositing* out of natal strife. When dealing with hard and persistent natal aspects, it is quite useful to use composite energies to aid in releasing "issues of temperament" that have existed for many years. If a person has experienced an extremely hard childhood or is extremely sensitive for other reasons, then it will be even more crucial to engage relationships that are conducive to a brighter future. What the composite chart will indicate is how two people will feel if they are to merge with one another over time. When we think of merging, we often think of partnership in the marriage sense. But energetic merging can happen in a number of ways. The process of merging into a composite chart simply requires time, attention, and the sharing of needs, wills, desires, and language. The length of time it takes for two individuals to truly merge depends of course on the two people involved, as well as the level at which they are engaged with one another.

Astrocartography

Many astrologers specialize in Astrocartography, or the study of how our natal patterns mix with the energetics of certain locations on the globe. This technique assumes that the manner in which we "vibe with a certain city" can be very important to our happiness and prosperity in that location. At times, when a client is looking to move to a new town, and they are also trying to set a clear intention for life, Astrocartography can help in this endeavor. In this case, we could help our client find a city that will "vibe them right" in terms of what they are trying to accomplish. Another use of astrocartographic information would be to guide clients into "intentional merging" with a certain city or town. Suppose our client was found to be fatigued constantly, and we noticed that they are living in the town that sits upon their "Neptune line." In order to use this information in a fashion as to "remedy" the issue, we would encourage the client to move to a town where the energy would support the client's larger goal to feel better, be more vivacious, etc. For a situation such as this we may suggest that our client move to a town which sits upon their "Mars line" or "Sun line," the idea being that such locations would strengthen the vital forces in our otherwise sleepy client.

Gem Remedies

Historically, Vedic and Western astrologers alike have provided gem remedies for problems in the astrological chart. The assumption in using gems is that the vibrational nature of the gems themselves can be used to alter a person's field. For instance, if a person were to be born with a highly debilitated Venus, and the natal Venus was also found being hit by a hard transit, an astrologer would want to strengthen Venus. A gem remedialist would likely prescribe a Venusian stone to be worn through the duration of the transit.

In the modern day, gem healers are still hard at work. I recently discovered a gem remedialist in a very unlikely location...at a sign language interpreting assignment. It turns out that one of my colleagues in the field builds personal "gem grids." I showed up to work one day on a hard transit. My heart felt as if it was tight, as my psyche was deeply unsettled on this particular day. When I laid my eyes upon the gem grid she had brought to show me, it was as if the geometry of the stones realigned my understanding, my heartbeat. It was on this day that I came to understand the power of gem remedies. Regardless of how a gem remedialist does their work, the intent is similar—to strengthen and align a person's vibration, heart, intentions, and thinking.

Conclusion

Now that we have looked into some of the theory and methodology behind astrological remediation, the next step will be to integrate these ideas in our everyday practice. We might begin by asking ourselves a few pertinent questions. How will we attempt to lighten the load for our next client? What methods of remediation speak to us? How can we use the current time period for the greatest good? We may even try to utilize one of the methodologies presented here into our next few readings. Perhaps we do a little strategic planning for our client, try to channel their Mercury/Pluto conjunction into a worthy cause, or send them home with a flower essence. In each of these cases, we have made life a little better in the process. And this is the heart of astrological remediation.

ANDREA L. GEHRZ is an astrological scholar and teacher, based in Portland, OR. A true lover of the celestial clock, Andrea can often be found hand drawing astrological charts, reading the ephemeris, and attempting to maximize the outside influences of the transits. Currently, Gehrz focuses much of her spirit into running the Moira Press—a publishing company dedicated to crafting astrological textbooks, ancient and modern. When not thinking about astrology, Gehrz can be found playing public pianos, moonlighting as an ASL interpreter, and running wild with her ultra-Sagittarian daughter. Contact her at MoiraPress.org

---

Venus Envy

Photography *by* Wonder Bright

Venus does not get enough credit for what it signifies in the world. We think of it as something on the periphery, it's relegated to decoration and dismissed every bit as much as the women it symbolizes. But there's a reason religions spend so much money building churches and places like the Grand Canyon are a tourist destination. Beauty, great beauty, instills awe in us. It inspires us and lifts us up. It gives us a connection to spirit and to being a part of something larger than ourselves.

Venus is the planet we turn to when we look for love in a chart but even here our cultural beliefs about love color our experience of this planet. In her book *Illuminata* Marianne Williamson observed our culture thinks falling in love is a delusional state and that it's only when we fall out of love that the scales fall from our eyes and we see the other as he or she really is. She says this is completely backwards, and in fact it's falling in love that allows us to see the other as they really are. It's then that we see him or her without judgment and through the eyes of the Divine. So it's only when we fall *in love* that we see the Other as Divine, and that is actually the Truth, capital T, of the experience, and maybe of any experience.

I am on a quest to look at everyone I meet through this prism. I can't claim success even most of the time but just the attempt is rendering my life more beautiful and hallowed. *Venus Envy* is a portrait series featuring people I meet who have a way of connecting, loving, and/or expressing beauty in ways that inspire me to do it better or come at it from an angle new to me.

¶ I'm very forceful, and bossy, but people sort of like that. (*laughs*)…because people really like having someone who has an idea, "let's do something!" with enthusiasm, which I have a lot of. Because I like engaging in the world in a whole lot of different ways. How I actually connect with people, is that we're going to do something together, I've been a central figure in getting people to do stuff, you know, "let's go to the ocean" in the middle of the night, and…(*laughs*) stuff like that, …I think I always was a core person for getting people to do things, because I'm a doer, I *do* stuff. I just really enjoy life.

Mary Passmore: *Scorpio Venus opposite Taurus Moon in the 10th house*

I took this photo of my mother, Mary, sitting at the window watching the sun rise in the Himalayan mountains when she took me there in 2012.

♀

Gustavo Cendejas: *Libra Venus sextile Uranus and Jupiter in Sagittarius*

I took this picture of Gustavo just after dawn in Elysian Park above Los Angeles. Gustavo moved to Los Angeles when he was fifteen, he grew up in Mexico City. He was raised Catholic.

¶ We focus on superficial stuff, and we don't look beyond that, we don't really pay attention to what's behind that. So I guess that's why we don't see beauty all the time. I think so. We're not using our heart to look for it, just the eyes. And we don't get a chance to just go deeply and find real beauty. We don't allow ourselves to just be ourselves, and

I think that's the beauty, it's being ourselves, and finding that, because we're all beautiful. You're beautiful. I'm beautiful. …You know maybe that's the first thing, when you find that beauty inside you.

That happened for me after I got my freedom. Being gay, coming out. That was like a big step and that's when I feel free. That was beautiful. That was a big breakthrough in my life. And that was beautiful. That was a good moment. (laughs) That was the first time I saw beauty. It felt like freedom to me. I was allowed to be myself, I was allowed to be who I am. I didn't have to lie anymore, I didn't have to be somebody I wasn't because I was living a different life. And now it's me. So I guess that's beautiful.

♀

LESTER ROQUE: *Sagittarius Venus in mutual reception with Jupiter in Libra*

I took this photograph of Lester at his home in Silverlake. Lester got his first tattoo when he quit working in advertising seven years ago at the beginning of the recession, a corporate career that spanned 32 years.

¶ I've always been able to have a feeling about certain times. I kinda think that's what the Venus thing is about: being able to accept change and always land on your feet. You're like, one with the, I don't know if it's the planets, or whatever it is, you know? I don't know, who knows? …A lot of people get an overwhelming feeling, and things work out for them, no matter what it is… You feel like… just, let it run all over your body and embrace it and feel it. Because it's going to be OK. It might look like it's dark, but if you can ride it out, I just have this feeling, and I seem to be OK.

…for me this look is very peaceful. People seem to invite me *more* into their lives, 'cause I have little old ladies that come to me, they're supposed to be scared, but they ain't. They're sort of touching my arm, "oh I like your tattoo," or "why would you do that to yourself? Didn't that hurt? Are you a wrestler?" And it seems to open up a dialogue for people. It doesn't close them up. I'm very inviting. If you start

ALYCE BONURA: *Leo Venus opposite Saturn in Aquarius, Libra Rising*

I took this photograph of Alyce for the book cover of her memoir, Mother Rabbit about her time as a den mother to Playboy Bunnies in the 1960's. Alyce currently owns a thriving business as a tax accountant.

¶ I get up in the morning and I don't want to go to work, I say, "Ok, I gotta go to work, and I say, first things first let me start something. I never let a day go by even if I don't feel good. What's that got to do with anything? (*laughs*) Anything? This morning I got up and I didn't want to do anything and I wasn't feeling that great, and I sat down and I figured it out and I said, "well, I better get going," and I do. And then I do the whole day. I get by that. Every day I get by that. I can feel, "oh my god, somebody's let me down, Oh my god look what's happening, Oh this is a disaster, I want to go back to bed," but I don't. I just plod on.

♀

touching me in the supermarket I'm not going to say "now stop that." I knew what I was doing when I was getting tattooed and looking different and whatnot.

I was on the train to San Diego once and there was this tattooed kid in front of me and this other guy started talking about this guys tatts, and then the guy with the tatts said, "oh I don't want to talk to you, I just want to be left alone, I'm just like everybody else," and I said, "dude, *you're not!* Look at you, you're tattooed, you're pierced like me! If you didn't do this to draw attention to yourself, you shouldn't have done it!"

So that's how I feel about it, if you don't want to be bothered, have people coming up to you, don't look so different. Don't make that choice. You made the choice. Especially when you got the tattooed head and the piercings. My gosh, I was talking to him on the train, "Dude, you're an idiot! You should. not. have. done. that." (*laughs*)

Leslie Jordan: *Scorpio Rising, Aries Venus sextile Mars in Gemini*

I took these photographs of Leslie at his home in Los Angeles. Leslie is an Emmy award winning actor and writer currently touring the world performing his one-man show detailing his love affairs with young straight men he's known. It's called "Cheese, My Love Affair with the Camera."

¶ You know, I think we *need* to be surrounded by beauty 'cause there's so much ugliness in the world (laughs) there's just *so much* ugliness in the world. My dream, my ultimate dream is to buy a pony farm. There's an island of the coast of Virginia, Chincoteague Island, and they don't know if a Spanish galleon sunk in the 1700s or what, but these horses swam to this island and for 89 years the fire department has swum over and culled the herd and swims them to the mainland and gentles them and sells them at the big pony auction. But then people ride them and stuff and I want to return them to the *wild*, I want to buy land in Tennessee, and wherever and I want to have a *pony farm* (chuckles) with *wild* Chincoteague horses, they're gorgeous!

Take something like that and return it to the wild—return things to the way they are. You know, leaving things, letting things be as they are.

Lisa O'Hare: *Libra Venus in the 10th house*

I took this photo of Lisa relaxing in the evening on vacation in Topanga Canyon. Lisa is a singer and actor currently starring in the Broadway hit "A Gentleman's Guide to Love and Murder"

¶ When I think about what is beautiful it's always nature, being amongst trees, being with nature makes me feel grounded and whole in a way that nothing else does. When I'm in the city for too long I don't feel very grounded, I don't feel very close to myself, my heart feels—you know, when I get into nature it just makes me feel, it's just so beautiful in my mind, you know, being near the ocean, or being on a mountain top, there's just something about that, because it's made by God. Man made things can be very beautiful, but something that's just, you know, imperfect, it's the imperfections that make it so beautiful. No two trees are the same, no two waves are the same, and that's what makes things beautiful.

Even though you can look at a person that has a perfectly symmetrical face and think that it's beautiful, for me that's not what I'm drawn to, even in people, it's people with more quirky characteristics that I think are more interesting, but then I critique myself and want myself to be that idea of beautiful that it's never going to be, but it's like I can't see my own imperfection as being beautiful, but that's how I view others, which is very strange. I mean, I can also appreciate beautiful people that are societies idea of beautiful people, like models or actresses, I get it, but I don't think it's what I'm, like, when I'm just sitting on the subway in New York and I'm people watching, there's so much beauty in people, who are unaware that they're being watched and they're just kind of being, I love that. I love watching people just being. You know what it is? It's people that are authentic, people that are just true to themselves. I think the most unattractive thing to me is when someone is just trying too hard to be something.

It's really unattractive. It's a lesson. No matter how much you think you may be imperfect, it's those imperfections that people find interesting and attractive in you.

Wonder Bright is an astrologer and photographer living in Los Angeles. Her 12th house Capricorn Venus trines Saturn in Taurus and rules her 9th house Libra Moon. Her portrait series *Venus Envy* showed for the first time at ISAR's 2014 conference in Arizona. You can find more portraits and longer interviews at www.starsofwonder.com

Cosmos and Chaos:
Perpetual Tides *of the* Venus-Mars Epoch
An Astro-historiographical Documentary Essay, Part I
by Gary P Caton

> "A twofold tale I shall tell: at one time it grew to be one alone out of many, at another again it grew apart to be many out of one. Double is the birth of mortal things and double their failing…and these things never cease their continual exchange, now through Love all coming together into one, now again each carried apart by the hatred of Strife."
> – Empedocles of Acragas, Greek pre-Socratic philosopher, 5th Century BCE[1]

I BEGIN OUR TWOFOLD TALE in what is commonly called the cradle of Civilization, the fertile crescent of Mesopotamia. It was here the first extant recorded observations of planetary cycles occurred, in the Venus Tablet of Ammisaduqa. Over centuries upon centuries of climbing their ziggurats and recording what they witnessed in the Heavens, Mesopotamian astrologers amassed enough information about the movements of the planets to make possible the successful prediction of their placements. Thus we have the birth of ephemerides and indeed the theory of planetary motion initially used by Ptolemy in his *Almagest*.[2] "*At one time it grew to be one alone out of many.*" It was the many centuries of observations by Mesopotamian astrologers that made possible the birth of horoscopic astrology, the one form of astrology that has persisted throughout the life of Western Civilization since the Hellenistic era.

"*At another (time) again it grew apart to be many out of one.*" As post-modern astrologers, even within the still primary horoscopic view, we often find ourselves with a plethora of schools of thought and techniques with which to ply our trade. Frequently this seems to result in a cacophony of seemingly irreconcilable voices. However, this relativistic noise should not be taken to imply that our *Ars Magna* is without a clear signal, emanating from elemental first principles. As the philosopher and astrologer Richard Tarnas notes, the great paradox of post-modern relativism is that ultimately it must be applied to itself.[3] This seems to imply a kind of philosophical double negative, wherein the multitudinous voices of relativism are canceled out as the chorus is turned back upon itself. Indeed, this is what Empedocles seems to be telling us in the opening epigraph: "*And these things never cease their continual exchange.*" Dealing with the fundamental philosophical problem of "the one and the many," Empedocles asserts that existence itself is a perpetual cycle between singularity and multiplicity. Thus, we should be able to find our way back to first principles.

This search for astrological first principles carries the patina of righteousness, yet it seems to be dominated, over the last twenty years or so, by a popular movement toward recovery and translation of Hellenistic and Medieval horoscopic astrological source texts. This is important work, to be sure, yet, in my view, it seems even more vital to the pursuit of elemental principles for astrologers to recover and reintroduce to modern astrology the most basic observational and astronomical skills and the fundamental cyclical knowledge of the Mesopotamian era—which made the birth of horoscopic astrology possible. Some have initiated the process of uncovering and expanding upon these cyclical origins of astrology, but this has yet to receive the same kind of generalized press and support as the horoscopic translation movement. Thus, a relatively vast and unexplored frontier waits to be re-discovered and further refined.

Classical astrology, at least since the Persian era, has long recognized astro-historical cycles related to the conjunctions of the slow moving planets Jupiter and Saturn.[4] However, many, if not most, astrologers are unaware that important longer cycles of the faster moving so-called "personal" planets also exist. For instance, it is at least 46, often 79, and as much as 125 years before Mercury will station in the same degree of the zodiac, 251 years before Venus does so, and 79, 204, or 489 years for Mars.[5]

Often it is said that because the orbital cycles of the invisible outer planets match or dwarf the entire human life cycle, that they must therefore symbolize trans-personal and/or transcendent functions. And yet the so-called personal planets exhibit cycles of similar, if not greater length, albeit in a less obvious fashion—to our modern eyes. From my experience and research I have found that, when we look deeper we can find a clear trans-personal and/or transcendent element inherent to the faster moving visible planets. For example, when we closely examine the long-term interactions of Venus and Mars—the two planets closest to

Earth—a cycle emerges that is two to three times the length of the Uranus-Pluto cycle. This new understanding of the Venus-Mars cycle has enormous potential significance for modern astrological understanding.

Literature Review

The primary modern source on the Venus-Mars cycle is *Cycles of Becoming* by Alexander Ruperti.[6] In the fourth chapter Ruperti lays out a 77-month cycle wherein every fifth conjunction of Venus-Mars occurs during Venus retrograde. Within this 77-month cycle, the conjunction with Venus retrograde is also part of a series of three conjunctions, what I call a "triple conjunction"—with all three conjunctions occurring during the span of only about nine months. These triple conjunctions are highlighted in the figure below. Though Ruperti did not spell it out, I have noticed that another defining part of this 77-month fractal is that three Venus-Mars oppositions take place between these sets of their triple conjunctions.

	Aspect	Date	Time	P1 Pos.	
	♀ - ☌ ♂	10-13-1933	05:30 pm	03°♐11'	
	♀ - ☌ ♂	01-24-1934	03:03 pm	21°♒49' ℞	
(1)	♀ - ☌ ♂	08-02-1934	11:09 am	11°♋53'	
	♀ - ☍ ♂	03-16-1935	07:24 am	22°♈46'	2325 days
(2)	♀ - ☌ ♂	06-19-1936	11:59 pm	26°♊09'	332 weeks
	♀ - ☍ ♂	06-27-1937	02:04 am	19°♉32'	76.5 months
(3)	♀ - ☌ ♂	05-07-1938	06:16 pm	09°♊45'	6 years,
	♀ - ☍ ♂	07-31-1939	05:58 am	27°♋23'	4 months,
(4)	♀ - ☌ ♂	04-09-1940	06:15 pm	05°♊25'	13 days
(5)	♀ - ☌ ♂	06-06-1940	11:35 pm	13°♋15' ℞	
(1)	♀ - ☌ ♂	12-03-1940	01:03 am	08°♏16'	
	♀ - ☍ ♂	09-09-1941	02:32 pm	23°♎39'	2345 days
(2)	♀ - ☌ ♂	10-23-1942	07:08 pm	24°♎01'	335 weeks
	♀ - ☍ ♂	01-07-1944	02:44 am	04°♐55'	77 months
(3)	♀ - ☌ ♂	09-10-1944	04:07 am	08°♎00'	6 years,
	♀ - ☍ ♂	01-16-1946	12:24 pm	22°♑12'	5 months,
(4)	♀ - ☌ ♂	08-08-1946	09:21 pm	29°♍43'	1 day
(5)	♀ - ☌ ♂	11-07-1946	03:35 am	00°♐26' ℞	
	♀ - ☌ ♂	05-18-1947	02:41 am	27°♈52'	
	♀ - ☍ ♂	01-22-1948	10:48 pm	06°♓12'	

Ruperti suggests that we focus our attention on the conjunction that occurs during Venus retrograde because it represents an opportunity to adjust (retrograde) the way our values (Venus) inform our actions (Mars). Thus, it seems about every six and a half years, there will arise a natural impulse to make adjustments between our desire nature (Venus) and how we are acting on it (Mars). Indeed, studies have shown quantitative correlations to the now famous "seven year itch."[7] There are of course several astrological factors that could be associated with a seven year cycle, including the transit of Uranus through a sign and the quartile or square within the Saturn and the progressed Lunar cycles; however, Venus and Mars are more fundamentally associated with relationships. As archetypes of "falling in love" and "breaking up," the Venus-Mars cycle is the most clearly related astrological indicator to this seven-year relationship cycle. Thus, the existent theory on the Venus-Mars cycle seems to make good sense, and Ruperti's advice would probably be a very practical way to experience this cycle psychologically—if only the cycle actually behaved this way currently!

	Aspect	Date	Time	P1 Pos.	
	♀ - ☌ ♂	04-09-1940	06:15 pm	05°♊25'	
	♀ - ☌ ♂	06-06-1940	11:35 pm	13°♋15' ℞	
(1)	♀ - ☌ ♂	12-03-1940	01:03 am	08°♏16'	2325 days
	♀ - ☍ ♂	09-09-1941	02:32 pm	23°♎39'	332 weeks
(2)	♀ - ☌ ♂	10-23-1942	07:08 pm	24°♎01'	76.5 months
	♀ - ☍ ♂	01-07-1944	02:44 am	04°♐55'	6 years,
(3)	♀ - ☌ ♂	09-10-1944	04:07 am	08°♎00'	4 months,
	♀ - ☍ ♂	01-16-1946	12:24 pm	22°♑12'	13 days
(4)	♀ - ☌ ♂	08-08-1946	09:21 pm	29°♍43'	
(5)	♀ - ☌ ♂	11-07-1946	03:35 am	00°♐26' ℞	
(1)	♀ - ☌ ♂	05-18-1947	02:41 am	27°♈52'	
	♀ - ☍ ♂	01-22-1948	10:48 pm	06°♓12'	2326 days
(2)	♀ - ☌ ♂	04-02-1949	09:14 pm	09°♈26'	332 weeks
	♀ - ☍ ♂	04-28-1950	07:51 am	22°♍10'	76.5 months
(3)	♀ - ☌ ♂	02-16-1951	11:03 am	19°♓42'	6 years,
	♀ - ☍ ♂	05-10-1952	01:42 am	07°♉15'	4 months,
(4)	♀ - ☌ ♂	01-17-1953	03:05 pm	13°♓48'	14 days
(5)	♀ - ☌ ♂	03-21-1953	09:16 pm	01°♉19' ?	
	♀ - ☌ ♂	10-04-1953	00:51 am	12°♍17'	
	♀ - ☍ ♂	05-30-1954	06:09 am	08°♋14'	

It turns out that the 77-month cycle which Ruperti codified only operates with regularity for about 200 years. The end of the most recent 200-year period occurred in the mid-1940s, and during the past 48 years—since 1966—there have been *only two* Venus-Mars conjunctions which occurred during Venus retrograde. The next one is due to occur August 31, 2015. What are we to make of this curious shift that has been hiding in plain sight?! What could be the ramifications of such a dramatic transformation within such a fundamental cycle?

In a blog post for *The Mountain Astrologer*, Robert Blaschke referred to this shift as a "century-long aberration in the Venus-Mars transit cycle, preceded by and followed by two centuries of regularity"—thus hinting at a larger cycle.[8] Blaschke also postulated that "social disruptions brought about by the changes to the relational patterns could take an entire century to stabilize." My research has found that the disruptive period itself lasts a full century, and then it takes the better part of two full centuries to once again reach maximum stabilization.

In her *The Sacred Dance of Venus and Mars*, Michele Finey contributes to a better understanding of the Venus-Mars epoch.[9] Finey groups the Venus-Mars conjunctions together by their 32-year longitudinal recurrence cycle (also mentioned by Ruperti), identifying further long term interactions—what she calls "Saros" series—in their activity. Essentially one can see long "strings" of consecutive 32-year conjunctions. These conjunctions recur near the same longitudinal or zodiacal position at each 32-year iteration, but slowly progress through the zodiac over long periods of time. The direct strings, or "saros," last for more than a thousand years and the retrograde strings, or "saros," last a few hundred years.

Finey then demonstrates that as some of these long conjunction strings or "saros" are ending, new ones are simultaneously beginning, and she postulates that it is at these transitional times of endings/beginnings that "the social fabric seems to be woven with different threads and materials." Finey tells us that "these 70–80 year periods of radical change don't happen very often, but we are living through one of them now." She never explicitly states how often these radical periods occur or recur, but implicit in her research is a 300-year cycle—what she calls a "retrograde saros cycle."

My own research

Recently, I conducted my own thorough investigation of the Venus-Mars cycle. I decided to undertake this arduous task during a series of three squares between Venus in Capricorn and Mars in Libra, made possible by their extended stays in these signs due to retrogrades therein. It should be noted that the transit placements under which I conducted my research constitute a kind of "mutual reception" in astrology. Capricorn is the place of Mars' exaltation and Libra is Venus' diurnal domicile. By being in each other's favored places and making an aspect, there is a special connection between Venus and Mars during this time. Via the Thema Mundi, it is the nature of a square (like Mars) to separate things and distinguish them one from another, so I found this particular time was ideal for this particular investigation. By separating the Venus-Mars interactions into two parts, the regularity described by Ruperti and the "aberration" described by Blaschke, I discovered a fundamental 300-year cycle in their interactions. This epochal cycle was confirmed going back at least seven iterations, that is, over more than two millennia of Venus-Mars conjunctions.

The 300 Year Venus-Mars Epoch

"In all chaos there is a cosmos, in all disorder a secret order"
—C.G. Jung "Archetypes of the Collective Unconscious"[10]

An in-depth study of the conjunctions between Venus and Mars clearly reveals an approximately 300-year cycle in the patterning of their conjunctions. This 300-year cycle consists of two distinct but unequal parts. There is a period of about 200 years which is comprised of very consistent and regular interactions between Venus and Mars, and there is an approximately 100-year period where the interactions become inconsistent and erratic. The phenomenological nature of these two periods corresponds to the orbital and archetypal qualities of the two planets. Moreover, it appears that substantial correspondences exist both within and between the historical trends associated with these two periods and the nature of the two planets as archetypes of love and strife, peace and war, cosmos and chaos. Thus, the 300-year Venus-Mars epoch can serve as an astro-historical meta-meme, that is, a tool for examining meme-plexes—groups of related ideas, behaviors, and/or styles which spread from person to person within a culture over time.

Defining Terms

The 200-year Venus period is composed of 32 consecutive iterations of the 77-month cycle described by Ruperti. Once again, the basic fractal consists of five Venus-Mars conjunctions, every fifth one occurring during Venus retrograde. This retrograde conjunction occurs as the middle of a set of three conjunctions, all three of which occur within a nine-month period. During this nine-month period, Venus and Mars do not achieve opposition, or even square relationship to each other. Basically Venus passes Mars, then about 100 to 200 days later (on average) Mars passes Venus, and 100 to 200 days later (on average) Venus passes Mars to make the third and final conjunction. After this triple conjunction, there are three complete cycles of ~700 days (on average), so that opposition is achieved three times between each set of triple conjunctions. This entire 77-month fractal repeats for 32 iterations, producing a period of about 205 years. The phenomenological nature of this ~200 year period is characterized by regular and consistent interactions. This is reflective of the nearly circular orbit of Venus and Her archetypal association with harmonious principles such as the Golden Mean. Thus, I have dubbed this 200 years the Venus period or era.

The 100-year period contains fewer conjunctions with Venus retrograde, as most of the conjunctions during this period occur with Venus stationary. During this shorter period there are 17–20 sets of triple conjunctions (as defined above). However, the triple conjunctions occur very erratically during this period, and at some point disappear altogether. Rather than the regular three oppositions between them, there can be as few as one and as many as six oppositions between sets of triple conjunctions during this shorter period. Furthermore, there are always one or two instances where the triple conjunction fails to perfect, and it is then that we see five or six oppositions occur between sets of triple conjunctions. At these times, one or two Venus-Mars cycles occur during which the interval between conjunctions stretches considerably—to approximately 940 days. Overall, we can see that the phenomenological nature of this 100-year period is inconsistent, irregular and characterized by the maximum duration of separation for the two bodies. This is reflective of the nature of Mars, both His highly eccentric orbit and His archetypal nature which is dry and separative. Thus I call this 100 years the Mars period or era.

♀♂♀

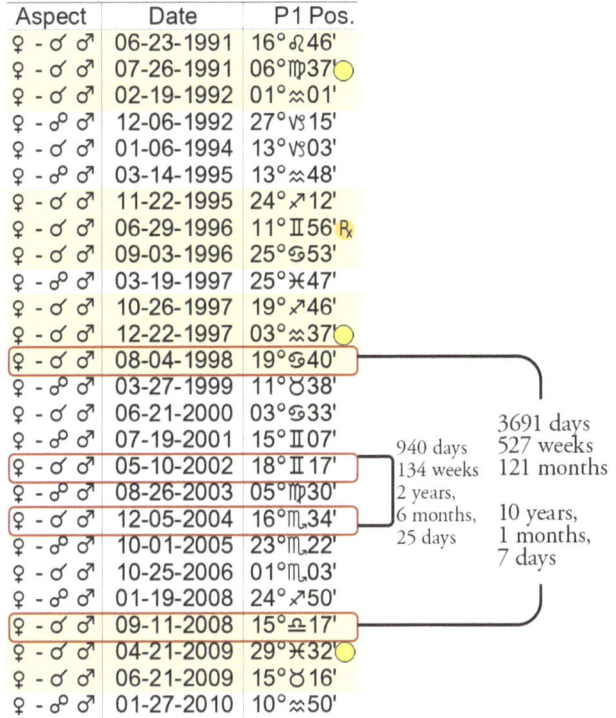

Synchronic Patterns

"If, for a moment, we look at (hu)mankind as one individual, we see that it is like a (person) carried away by unconscious powers."
—C. G. Jung (parentheses mine)[11]

In compiling the research for this documentary essay, I studied seven complete 300-year Venus-Mars epochs—spanning more than two millennia—from the time of the Roman Republic until present. Two kinds of patterns were observed. The first has to do with the synchronicity or "meaningful coincidence" of major historical events and trends happening *within* a particular 100- or 200-year period. Because these events and trends strongly correspond to the archetypal nature of the planet associated with that period, they go beyond simple coincidence into meaningful synchronicity. Thus, I will use a term coined by Richard Tarnas, and call these "synchronic patterns."[12]

The 200-year period or era is in archetypal accord with the nature of Venus and Her associations with cohesive and harmonious principles such as the Arts and the Golden Mean. It is often characterized by relative (especially internal) peace, social cohesion and order. This allows for the establishment and development of major and definitive socio-cultural meme-plexes. Due to its repetitive nature, often this period can be seen to contain a progressive pattern where new memes emerge toward the beginning of the period and gradually reach the height of their cohesion, expression, and significance toward the end of the period. Our first example can be seen in the expansion and dominance of the Roman Republic.

Historical Correspondences

Before applying astrology to the historical record, it is necessary to acknowledge that "periodization" of history has its own issues, and the terms are constantly being refined and updated. As we might expect, there exists substantial debate within the historical community itself on the nature and definition of long term historical periods. For instance, the term "Hundred Years War" is a modern invention used by some to refer to a series of related conflicts waged from 1337 to 1453—which is actually more than a hundred years! Some find the term more useful than others. As it turns out, this period coincides pretty closely to one of the 100-year radical Mars periods described above, which lasted from about 1347 to 1442. So, in this case the connection between astrology and history resonates quite closely. Nevertheless the reader should be cautioned against construing connections like this as "factual," "scientific," or any kind of "proof" of astrology.

Rather, the nature of archetypal associations is mythic, metaphorical, and poetic—and thus more artistic than scientific. As astrologers, we can use our craft to identify substantial trends and connections within the historical record—not only in an attempt to define a particular Zeitgeist or "spirit of the time" within a given period or era, but also to reveal new parameters for periodization. Therefore, what follows is best described as an astro-historiographical essay, wherein I primarily employ the poetic, expository, and participatory modes of documentary. I will attempt to convey the core Zeitgeist of each period in such a way as to demonstrate the larger astro-historical "sine wave" between cultural syntropy and entropy, which the Venus-Mars epoch appears to represent.

Era of Roman Expansion
(Venus period ~370–172 BCE)

After two centuries of class struggle between the patricians (aristocracy) and the plebeians (common freemen), the Lex Hortensia of 287 BCE granted the plebeians more power. This effectively ended plebeian secession as a political tool and formed a new patricio-plebeian senatorial aristocracy. The subsequent dominance of the senate established an internal order which minimized internal dispute and thus allowed for a focus on external issues of foreign and military policy. After the battle of Zama in 202 BCE, the other major Mediterranean power of Carthage was effectively eliminated. Rome then became the dominant power and established hegemony over the Mediterranean region. The establishment of internal peace and order and the subsequent concentration of political power and expansion of influence during this period all form a pattern consistent with the nature of Venus.

Era of Roman Republican Crisis
(Mars period ~167–78 bce)

The 100-year period is in archetypal accord with the nature of Mars and His associations with war, strife and division. Similar to its erratic nature, this period is often characterized by chaotic economic, social, and/or political circumstances as well as particularly destructive, decisive, and/or barbaric conflicts. In line with my thesis, historians often use the word "crisis" to describe these periods.

After establishing hegemony in the Mediterranean region, Roman political energy and eventually military might turned back upon itself. The period begins with the assassination of two political reformers, brothers by the name of Grachus. Though the deaths of the Gracchi may not technically equate by today's definition of the term, they were seen as *de facto* political assassinations.[13] This augured further internal turmoil.

The natural order of Roman politics was embodied in the *cursus honorum,* or "course of offices." This was a sequential order of public offices held by aspiring politicians with a minimum age requirement, minimum intervals between offices and repeating an office was forbidden. As these rules were altered and/or flagrantly ignored, instead of opportunities for public service, the offices often became more opportunities for self-aggrandizement.

For example, Gaius Marius held five consecutive consulships between 104 bce and 100 bce. Sulla saw Marius as a potential tyrant and sought to block him. Though Sulla passed reforms to the *cursus honorum*, in driving Marius out he also ultimately set the precedent for the end of the Republic—a Roman general marching upon Rome itself. Sulla's civil wars marked the height of this Mars period. On November 1 of 82 bce at the battle of the Colline Gate, just outside of Rome, over 50,000 combatants lost their lives. Sulla stood alone as the master of Rome, the dictatorship revived. Sulla would in turn become the inspiration for both Pompey and Caesar, thus he can essentially be seen as the early stirring of the seed which eventually becomes the office of Emperor.

Often there are no clear-cut ending/beginning dates in history and the transition from Roman Republic to Empire is an example. Many historians mark the end of the Roman Republic with the accession of Julius Caesar or Octavian/Augustus, however, when we look through the lens of the Venus-Mars epoch, it becomes clear that Sulla's brutal dictatorship at the end of this Mars period was effectively also the end of anything Republican. Both Sulla's marches on Rome and his bloody purges can be seen as tipping points from which Rome was never to return. Roman politics descends into mass assassination plots (Catilene) and secret alliances (1st Triumvirate). The assassinations, violations of *cursus honorum*, civil wars and bloody purges during this period all form a pattern consistent with the nature of Mars.

Era of Pax Romana
(Venus period ~71bce–127 ce)

The energy of Mars spills over into the beginning of this period, but Caesar's assassination did nothing to restore the Republic. The movement toward a new order could not be stopped. The Principate became a way for the Emperor to keep the appearance of the Republic and can be seen as essentially a period of "enlightened absolutism." With the Emperor being styled as *princeps* or "first citizen," there was a sense that the title was earned on the basis of merit, or *auctoritas*. Augustus reinforced this image by closing the Gates of Janus (the Roman ceremony to mark World Peace) three times, more than in all of prior Roman history.

Just as the expansion of the Roman Republic led to a crisis, the establishment of the Principate provided the political stability for Rome to expand once again. Arts, architecture, and commerce all greatly flourished, and in this sense the Pax Romana can be seen as a kind of Renaissance. The period ends with the first three of what became known as the five Good Emperors. The Empire reached the height of its expansion under Trajan, the first Emperor born outside of Italy. At the end of this period the Roman Empire stretched across Europe, the Middle East, and North Africa. It would never be bigger. The establishment of the Principate, the closing of the Gates of Janus, the flourishing of arts and commerce, and the expansion of influence during this period all form a pattern consistent with the nature of Venus.

Era of Two Emperors
(Mars period ~132–221ce)

Some historians extend the Pax Romana through the reign of the five Good Emperors, as Marcus Aurelius is generally seen as a kind of reflection of Plato's utopian vision of a philosopher-king. Though it does seem clear that Marcus Aurelius was a good man, the reality is that his reign was very troubled. To begin with, he was not sole Emperor, but co-Emperor with his adoptive brother Lucius Verus. This was the first time Rome was ruled by two Emperors—a practice which would become much more common, especially in centuries to come.

There were floods, famine, and, by the year 167, successful invasions by multiple Germanic tribes. The Parthian War brought with it what became known as the Antonine plague. Marcus Aurelius actually had to bargain with the Germanic tribes to re-settle border areas of the Empire that were ravaged by plague in order to achieve peace.

By the year 189 it is said that the plague was killing 2,000 per day in Rome. In addition, there was a crisis of leadership. Marcus Aurelius' heir Commodus went insane with megalomania and was assassinated. This led to political chaos and "the Year of the Five Emperors." Things went downhill further from there with brother murdering brother to become sole Emperor (Caracalla). The division of the office of Emperor, Germanic invasions, plague, chaotic politics, Imperial insanity, and murder during this period all form a pattern consistent with the nature of Mars.

Christian Era
(Venus period ~222–432ce)

The early part of this period was colored by the chaos of the preceding Mars period. This has generally been called the "Crisis of the Third Century" and is seen to have ended in 284 with Diocletian, a man of low birth who rose through the ranks of the military. By appointing fellow military officer Maximian as co-Emperor, Diocletian formally divided the Empire into East and West, with an Augustus (senior co-Emperor) and Caesar (junior or deputy co-Emperor) for each, forming what is now called the Tetrarchy. This lasted until 313, leaving Constantine in the East and Licinius in the West as co-Emperors.

Constantine was the first Christian Emperor and played an influential role in the proclamation of the 313 Edict of Milan, which decreed religious tolerance throughout the empire. Halfway through this period, by 324, Constantine became sole ruler of both West and East. The solidus, a new gold coin, was introduced and would become the standard currency for more than a thousand years. Constantine called the First Council of Nicaea in 325, at which the Nicene Creed was professed by Christians. In 330 Constantine built a new imperial residence at Byzantium and named it "New Rome" or *Deutera Rhome* "Second Rome." However, it became known as Constantinople, and would later be the capital of what is now known as the Byzantine Empire for over one thousand years.

It was not until 380 under Theodosius that Christianity became the official Roman state religion. Theodosius was the last Emperor to rule a united Empire. To cement the status of Christianity as State religion, he dissolved the order of the Vestal Virgins in Rome, and in 393, he banned the pagan rituals of the Olympics in Ancient Greece. It was not until the end of the nineteenth century, in 1896, that Olympics were held again. After his death in 395, Theodosius' sons Arcadius and Honorius inherited the East and West halves respectively, and the Roman Empire was never again re-united. The establishment of a standard currency, a State religion and a new Imperial capital during this period (all three of which will endure for a thousand years or more), these all form a pattern consistent with the nature of Venus.

Germanic Era
(Mars period ~432–533ce)

This period is characterized in the West both by Roman descent and the ascendancy of Germanic peoples in their place. This was happening all along the northern and western frontiers of the Roman Empire. Much more than a simple power shift, this represents a marked cultural shift as well. The Anglo-Saxon settlement of Britain brought with it Old English as the dominant language and the replacement of Roman masonry with a wooden material culture, with concern for trees and timber showing from cups to halls and in Anglo-Saxon place-names, literature, and religion. These were tribal people with local and extended kin groups being the essential cultural unit.

On the mainland this period sees the end of the Western Roman Empire. The second sack of Rome in 455 by the Vandals is seen as a turning point, as well as the rise of the Germanic Kings, Odoacer and Theodoric. Odoacer became the first King of Italy, replacing the Roman Emperors. Despite being a capable ruler, Odoacer was unable to defeat the Ostrogoths and their monarch, Theodoric. In seemingly perfect synchronicity, the epic clash between these two "barbarian" Kings commenced during the height of the Mars period. Between 484 and 494 the triple conjunctions between Venus and Mars disappear, and are replaced by a series of five consecutive oppositions and the longest interval possible between Venus-Mars conjunctions. After four years of intense fighting, Odoacer surrendered. It is said that later Theodoric murdered Odoacer with his own hands at an ostensibly peaceful feast, and eventually all of Odoacer's family and most of his army were murdered as well. The Anglo-Saxon settlements, Germanic invasions, epic conflict, and royal murder during this period all form a pattern consistent with the nature of Mars.

Furthermore, this period is generally seen as the division between the much larger historical periods of Classical Antiquity and the Middle Ages, both of which lasted about a thousand years each. As such, the basic nature of Mars—to separate one thing from another—is palpably visible here. This particular separation is a most profound one. This division of Europe between the Romans in the East and the Germanic tribes in the West reverberates through the coming eras, echoing for more than a thousand years, well into the twentieth century, pointing us to a new kind of pattern emerging in our historiography.

Diachronic Patterns

At the crux of two very large periods, Classical Antiquity and the Middle Ages, we are at a major dividing line in the historical tapestry. As we compare these individual Venus and Mars periods to others of the same nature, we can identify another kind of pattern in our historiography—one that Tarnas called "diachronic patterns."[14] Just as the historical fabric shows synchronic patterns *within* a given period—i.e., notable wars and chaotic events happening during the 100 years associated with Mars—we can also see patterns in the historical fabric reverberating *across* periods, so that we see similar themes, or a continuation of a theme, during subsequent periods of the same nature.

"Scorpio," by Nick Gucker, for the CONSTELLATION art show

"When taking on the concept of Scorpio for the CONSTELLATION exhibit curated by Yvette Endrijautzki, I wanted to convey something more complex in my study than the traditional, straightforward Scorpion image. As I considered the symbol of Scorpio, the ideas of fearlessness, determination and strength were the primary elements impressed upon me. I wanted to focus on the aspect of strength, so I incorporated the traditional image of the scorpion into that of an old fashioned circus strong man, replacing his arms with scorpion tails. It seemed a perfect fit, in a classic strong-man pose. As Scorpio is a water sign, I wanted to incorporate water elements into the image as well. I originally intended to have the elephants spraying fountains of water, but once they came into form, the trunk shape lent itself to more scorpion tails; a fun indulgence in studying the creature's anatomy. The third eye (the eye of knowledge) on the elephants' fez is meant to instill a sort of playful mysticism."
—*Nick Gucker*

☿

For instance, we have outlined three Venus periods thus far. In accord with the regularity and consistency of their alignments, all three of the Venus periods have a cohesive quality where political power becomes more concentrated and eventually forms a singularly dominant power or hegemony. Furthermore, across these three Venus periods a pattern emerges. The dominant power or hegemony moves from being embodied primarily in the Senate in the first Venus period, then moves to the office of Emperor in the second, and finally political power moves to being invested in The Church by the third Venus period. Eventually we will see this pattern further extended until the office of Pope ultimately becomes a dominant influence in state politics throughout the Middle Ages. Thus we can see how the cohesive and unitary nature of Venus results in diachronic patterns where subsequent Venus periods can be seen to distill political power into new forms of Hegemony.

Similarly, we can see diachronic patterns across the various Mars periods we have covered thus far. The Germanic invasions which Marcus Aurelius could not completely repel during the Mars period I have dubbed "the Era of Two Emperors" ultimately became a tidal wave which completely overcame the Western Empire in the subsequent Mars period dubbed the "Germanic Era." It has also not been lost on historians that the Antonine plague (of the Mars period I have called "the Era of Two Emperors") helped plant the seeds for the later Fall of the Western Empire in the subsequent Mars period ("the Germanic Era").[15]

Taking an even larger view and going back to the beginning of our investigation, we can see a diachronic pattern across all three Mars periods investigated so far. The internal conflicts of opposites between the Gracchi/Senate and Marius/Sulla during the first Mars period were subsequently externalized. In the second Mars period the primary opposition becomes that of Roman/Barbarian, and by the third Mars period this externalization of conflict becomes an overwhelming barbarian horde. Thus we can see the divisive nature of Mars in the diachronic pattern of a continual breaking apart of the dominant Hegemony during the Mars periods.

When viewed as a progression like this, it seems as if the basic nature of the 300-year Venus-Mars epoch can serve not only as a base unit for historiography—but perhaps it may also function as an *alembic maximus,* or a macrocosmic alembic—a kind of alchemical vessel for cultures. The basic alchemical formula is *Solve et Coagula*, which means "break apart and put back together." It appears the meme-stuff of cultures may be made to obey similar alchemical principles as the organic life-cycle. After a period of time, perhaps the old, brittle, dried out remnants of the once vital meme-stuff can be periodically broken down and recycled in order to re-fecundate and re-birth the culture. And yet, ultimately it seems cultures too must have seasons of becoming and of passing away. Nothing lasts forever, certainly nothing human-made—or can it?

Synchronic Patterns

Islamic Era
(Venus period ~ 545–744CE)

As we resume our overview of the alternating Venus and Mars periods, and the previous Mars period gives way to a new Venus period, we see the beginning of an important movement known as *renovatio imperii* or sometimes *restauratio imperii*, meaning "rebirth (or restoration) of the Empire." This began as a movement by Justinian to literally regain the Western Empire territory that had been lost to the Germanic "barbarians," but these ideas will resurface in various more figurative forms by different peoples well into the twentieth century. Also, the general concept of a Renaissance will become common in the coming Venus periods.

Just as Justinian's rule straddled the transition from a Mars to a Venus period, we can see elements of both archetypal powers expressing themselves during his rule. Justinian realized a series of brilliant early military successes in the 530s, re-capturing much of the lost territory of the Western Empire. Later, as the Venus period begins we can also see a distinctive trend toward social order and cultural advance. His legacy includes standardization of Roman law via the *Corpus Juris Civilis*, which is still the basis of civil law in many modern states. His reign also saw development of Byzantine art and its construction program has left several architectural masterpieces, particularly the basilica Hagia Sophia, which was the center of eastern Christianity for several centuries.

In the end, Justinian's ambition to restore the Roman Empire to its former glory was only partly realized, and eventually entirely reversed. After a devastating outbreak of bubonic plague (known as the Plague of Justinian), the Empire struggled to maintain its recent gains and eventually entered a period of territorial decline not to be reversed until the ninth century. The greater part of Italy would be lost to the invading Lombards just three years after Justinian's death (568), Spania was completely recovered by the Visigoths in 624, and within a century and a half Africa would be forever lost for the empire to the Rashidun and Umayyad Caliphates during what became known as the Muslim conquests.

Like the scales of the constellation and sign Libra which are astrologically associated with Venus, the descent of the Byzantine Empire during this period was balanced by the ascent of a new one. The period known as the Muslim, Islamic, or Arab conquests, began with the Islamic prophet Muhammad in the seventh century. He established a new unity in the Arabian Peninsula under which the subsequent Rashidun and Umayyad Caliphates saw a century of rapid expansion. This grew well beyond the Arabian Peninsula in the form of a Muslim Empire that stretched from the borders of China and India, across the Middle East and North Africa, and into Central Asia and Europe. The Muslim expansion was only halted at the failed siege of Constantinople in 717–718 and the battle of Tours in 732, preserving Christianity in Europe. Nevertheless, this expansion is generally seen to have initiated an Islamic Golden Age starting with the Abbasid Caliphate in the mid–eighth century and lasting until the Mongol conquest of Baghdad in 1258. Both Justinian's ultimately unsuccessful attempts at restoring the Western Empire and the ultimately successful establishment of the Muslim Empire during this period form a pattern consistent with the nature of Venus.

Carolingian Era
(Mars period ~748–844CE)

As this era opens the last Umayyad caliph is overthrown in 750 and the Caliphate is moved to Baghdad. Meanwhile in the West, the Viking age commences. The first official records of Vikings in England are passages in the Anglo Saxon Chronicle from 787, and in 793 the marauders destroyed the coastal monastery at Lindisfarne. In near perfect synchronicity, the Viking appearance was during the height of the Mars period, when the triple conjunctions between Venus and Mars disappear, and are replaced by a series of five consecutive oppositions and the longest interval between Venus-Mars conjunctions for the entire 300-year Epoch. We can also see diachronic patterns here: yet another overwhelming barbarian horde emerges during a Mars period—evocative of the Germanic and Viking invasions—and the Anglo-Saxon settlement of Britain during the previous Mars period parallels the Viking raids of the same island in the subsequent Mars period.

Another diachronic pattern emerges as the Saxons once again play a central role in a Mars period, but now it is they who are overcome. While the Vikings raid the coasts, on the mainland Charlemagne battles with the Saxons for 32 years (a basic Venus-Mars interval). Charlemagne emerges victorious in the Saxon Wars, incorporating Saxony into the Frankish realm and converting them to Christianity. In that sense, this can be seen as the first Holy War, and a precursor to the first Crusade of the next Mars period—setting up yet another diachronic pattern.

Perhaps as a reward for his conversions, Charlemagne is crowned Emperor by the Pope in 800. This was actually an especially divisive act. Rather than, or in addition to, reclaiming the title of Emperor of the Western Empire, Pope Leo III and Charlemagne could be seen as effectively claiming the title of Emperor of all Rome—thus nullifying the legitimacy of Empress Irene of the East in Constantinople. This led to centuries of competing claims between West and East of sovereignty over the whole Empire. Furthermore, the establishment of Charlemagne as Emperor elect, chosen by the Pope, sets up the eventual conflict between Emperor and Pope for supreme power—the ultimate effects of which would become known as the Investiture Controversy during the subsequent Mars period.

Finally, the coronation of Charlemagne as Emperor began what became known as the Holy Roman Empire and re-formalized the *translatio imperii* (transfer of rule) principle in the West. The (Germanic) Holy Roman Emperors were thus regarded as the inheritors of the title of Emperor of the Western Roman Empire, a title left unclaimed in the West after the death of Julius Nepos in 480 (at the height of the previous Mars period). Fundamental to the prestige of the Holy Roman Emperor was the notion that the Emperor held a supreme power which was inherited from the old emperors of Rome.

To Be, or Not to Be:
Being versus Becoming as Ontogeny Recapitulates Ontology

With the reappearance of the doctrine of *translatio imperii* into the historical tapestry, we enter into territory where we can begin to more clearly sense the presence of two competing visions of reality. On the one hand, we can see a need to assert a kind of unity with the past and a sense that the new is built directly upon the foundations of the old—in this case the Roman Empire. On the other hand, we will eventually see the emergence of a New World, new planets, and new technologies which seem to suggest a genuine departure from anything that had existed before.

Despite the coming influx of the New, the division of the Roman Empire into West and East has a ripple effect that can be seen continuing well into the twentieth century, if not until present day. Even after its fall in the West, the Roman Empire's cultural influence would formally continue through the Eastern or Byzantine Empire and would last another thousand years. In the East, the direct line of Roman Emperors (if ignoring Ottoman claims) ends with the Fall of Constantinople in 1453. However, within decades, Russian rulers (Ivan III) were seen to continue in the role of the Eastern Roman Emperors to whom they were related by blood and with whom they shared their orthodox Christian faith. Thus, (in the fashion of Constantine before) they saw Moscow to be a "New Rome" or the "Third Rome" and eventually took up the title of Emperor (Caesar or *Tsar*).

Via the Carolingians, the West becomes what is called the Holy Roman Empire, although Roman in name only. The term is used to denote the doctrine of *translatio imperii* or "transfer of rule," discussed previously. The core of the Holy Roman Empire centered on Germanic principalities and free states, and later the Nazis would eventually use this concept to legitimize their power historiographically, by portraying their ascendancy to rule as the direct continuation of an ancient and modern German past via the term *das Dritte Reich* meaning "the Third Reich"—or "the Third Empire."

Is it any wonder that these two competing visions of the inheritance of Roman Empirical authority came into conflict during WWII? More importantly, is that storyline finally and fully played out? When viewing history through the lens of the Venus-Mars epoch it becomes clear that Ontology—the ideas we have about the fundamental nature of existence—can be seen to be driving Ontogeny, or the development of the cultural storylines. If a singular Monadic Being dominates our Ontological views, then ultimately the nature of reality is fixed and constant—change is an illusion. Thus, we tend to create political storylines which reflect the fixed, constant and unchanging nature of reality. And yet, despite the seemingly overwhelming desire to assert a unity between the past, present and future, we can nevertheless also see clear dividing lines consistently emerge in our historiography. It seems as if there are two basic stories at work here.

In the second part of this essay we will look at a few of the ontological models provided by the pre-Socratic philosophers of Greece and see that there are indeed two contrasting models of reality which imply a fundamental divide between a static unity with the past and the dynamic emergence of the new. But we will also see that there is a third model which not only reflects a synthesis of these two competing models, but also very closely resembles the astronomical nature of the Venus-Mars epoch. These ideas will then inform our historiography of the remaining Epochs between the Carolingian era and the present, as well as any speculations as to what the future may hold.

Endnotes

In the interest of simplicity and brevity, I did not footnote anything that seemed to be relatively common knowledge and/or relatively widely accepted as historical fact. Notes are used only where I have quoted, made assertions that may not be a common point of view, or made references to specific facts, figures, or relatively specialized knowledge.

1 Richard Parry, "Empedocles," in *The Stanford Encyclopedia of Philosophy, edited by* Edward N. Zalta, (Fall 2012 Ed.): http://plato.stanford.edu/archives/fall2012/entries/empedocles

2 Sandra M. Caravella, "Triangles in the Sky: Trigonometry and Early Theories of Planetary Motion—Planetary Periods," *Loci*, New Jersey City University, (August 2010): http://www.maa.org/publications/periodicals/convergence/triangles-in-the-sky-trigonometry-and-early-theories-of-planetary-motion-planetary-periods

3 Richard Tarnas, *The Passion of the Western Mind: Understanding the Ideas That Have Shaped Our World View* (New York: Random House, 1991), p. 402.

4 Nicholas Campion wrote an excellent summary of the history of this technique in Bernadette Brady and Darrelyn Gunzburg's "Visual Astrology Newsletter": http://www.zyntara.com/VisualAstrologyNewsletters/van_Feb2011/VAN%20Feb2011.htm

A modern interpretation of these cycles is available here: http://divineinspirationastrology.com/books/elemental-wave-chronicles-the-jupiter-saturn-cycle/

For a list of Jupiter-Saturn conjunctions, see: Neil F. Michelson, *Tables of Planetary Phenomenon* (San Diego: ACS Publications, 1993), p. 91.

5 The modern astrologers to research these cycles in depth are Ruperti, Munkasey, and Blaschke. See: Alexander Ruperti, *Cycles of Becoming: The Planetary Pattern of Growth* (1978; reprinted by Port Townsend, WA: EarthWalk School of Astrology Publishing, 2005); Michael Munkasey, "Station Cycles"—an as yet unpublished research article shared with interested members of the community; Robert P. Blaschke, *Astrology A Language of Life: Volume 5—Holographic Transits* (Port Townsend, WA: EarthWalk School of Astrology Publishing, 2006).

6 Ruperti, *Cycles of Becoming*.

7 Most studies show that the risk of separation is low during the first months of a marriage; it then increases (after about three years), reaches a maximum (at around seven years) and thereafter begins to decrease. See: http://epc2012.princeton.edu/papers/120335

For those whose first marriage ends in divorce, the average time to separation is between 6.6 and 6.7 years. Only about 55% of marriages are past their fifteenth anniversary—i.e., have survived two seven year itches. See, R. Ellis & R. Kreider, "Number, Timing, and Duration of Marriages and Divorces: 2009," *Current Population Reports* (May 2011), p. 18. Retrieved from http://www.census.gov/prod/2011pubs/p70-125.pdf.

Between 1867 and 1977, data are available for the United States or portions thereof to calculate the median duration of marriage at time of decree. While considerable fluctuation occurred in the median duration of marriage over this 111-year period—the median duration ranged between 5.8 years (1950) and 8.3 years (1889, 1891, 1900 & 1901)—the overall average is very close to seven years. See, U.S. Department of Health and Human Services, "Duration of Marriage Before Divorce," *National Vital Statistics System* 21, no. 38 (1981), p. 22.

8 Robert P. Blaschke, "Aberrations in the Venus-Mars cycle" blog for *The Mountain Astrologer* website (August 9, 2010): http://mountainastrologer.com/tma/aberrations-in-the-venus-mars-cycle

9 Michele Finey, *The Sacred Dance of Venus and Mars* (Bournemouth, UK: The Wessex Astrologer, 2012).

10 C. G. Jung, "Archetypes of the Collective Unconscious," pp. 3–41 in *The Collected Works of C. G. Jung* 9.1, translated by R. F. C. Hull (Princeton, NJ: Princeton University Press, 1968). Here Jung is referencing the wise aspect of the Anima archetype, or the unconscious magical inner feminine aspect within a man, which at first appears to him as merely chaotic. To put the popular quote in context: "the anima and life itself are meaningless in so far as they offer no interpretation. Yet they have a nature that can be interpreted, for *in all chaos there is a cosmos, in all disorder a secret order*, in all caprice a fixed law, for everything that works is grounded on its opposite. It takes man's discriminating understanding, which breaks everything down into antinomial judgments, to recognize this. Once he comes to grips with the anima, her chaotic capriciousness will give him cause to suspect a secret order, to sense a plan, a meaning, a purpose over and above her nature…" (http://jungland.net/Library/EngArchColUn.htm)

11 C. G. Jung, "The Function of Religious Symbols," pp. 242–52, in *The Collected Works of C.G. Jung* 18, translated by R. F. C. Hull (Princeton, NJ: Princeton University Press, 1976). Here Jung discusses the International element of the Shadow archetype, saying the very same behavior which is politely covered up in the West is simply more openly, methodically and shamelessly applied in the East, so that—very much like a neurotic person's projections—what is seen as an exterior "evil" across the Iron Curtain is simply the unveiling of our own Western shadow, previously covered up.

12 Richard, Tarnas, *Cosmos and Psyche: Intimations of a New World View* (New York: Penguin, 2006).

13 Plutarch, *The Parallel Lives*, translated by Bernadotte Perrin (London: Loeb Classical Library edition, 1921).

Tiberius became tribune and sought land reform via the break-up of large plantations and granting of land to military veterans and the poor, who as property owners would then become eligible for military service. This law known as Lex Sempronia Agraria was blocked by the powerful senate, with whom Tiberius became adversarial. Eventually Tiberius and 300 of his supporters were massacred by a mob wielding stone and stave and their bodies thrown in the Tiber river in order to deny them funeral rites. Plutarch tells us "this is said to have been the first sedition at Rome, since the abolition of royal power, to end in bloodshed and the death of citizens." (http://penelope.uchicago.edu/Thayer/E/Roman/Texts/Plutarch/Lives/Tiberius_Gracchus*.html)

Tiberius' younger brother Gaius would share his fate a decade later. Gaius' social reforms were more radical and far wider reaching than those of his brother, as was his adversarial attitude toward the senate. The senate basically declared Gaius an enemy of state and issued what amounted to a license to kill. Pursued by a mob, Gaius committed suicide (killed by his servant). His head was ransomed and cut off. His body along with three thousand of his followers was thrown in the Tiber. (http://penelope.uchicago.edu/Thayer/E/Roman/Texts/Plutarch/Lives/Caius_Gracchus*.html)

14 Tarnas, *Cosmos and Psyche*.

15 It seems not uncommon for historians to view the Antonine plague as a precursor to the end of the Western Empire. See, for instance: Sabbatini & Fiorino, "The Antonine Plague & The Decline of the Roman Empire" *Journal of Infectious Diseases* 17, no. 4 (Dec., 2009): pp. 261–75; and J. F. Gilliam, "The Plague under Marcus Aurelius," *The American Journal of Philology* 82, no. 3 (Jul., 1961): pp. 225–51.

GARY P. CATON is an eclectic astrologer who embraces an organic, process-oriented approach of spiritual exploration, growth, and transformation via the living sky. After immersion in shamanism and tarot, Gary was initiated an astrologer in 1993 by a magnificent dream showing him the Sun-Venus cazimi. He later earned a BS in Counseling *summa cum laude* and has developed an idiosyncratic, multi-disciplinary astrological practice over twenty-one years. From 18–23 February 2015 he will be hosting the inaugural Sky Astrology Conference in Cape Eleuthera, Bahamas. Gary can be reached at www.dreamastrologer.com and gary@dreamastrologer.com.

Katie Grinnan, Astrology Orchestra, Performance at the Integratron, 2012; A LAND (Los Angeles Nomadic Division) production. (Image by Erich Koyama)

Astro *Orchestra*

Interactive Art *by* Katie Grinnan

The *Astrology Orchestra* is a system-based composition that uses astrology to map out my birth chart from the perspective of the planets in our solar system. Each chart is radically different from the next due to the planet's position in space. The planetary transits from these charts translate into strings and notes, each set of sounds representing a planetary perspective. A metronome serves as the conductor for the orchestra, which was modified to a ten beat time signature to accommodate the nine possible strings (to correlate with the nine planets, including demoted Pluto) that could cross a given zodiac sign. A bell rings on the tenth beat to signal that the performers should change signs. The performers begin with the sign of Aries and circumnavigate the zodiac playing the planetary transits. Within the ten beat time signature the performers can arrange the notes as they choose, leaving room for variation within each rotation. When the metronome stops, the performance ends. This performance is influenced by artists/composers such as John Cage, La Monte Young, and John Luther Adams.[1]

Katie Grinnan received her MFA from UCLA. She has had solo exhibitions at The Whitney Museum at Altria, the MAK Center and the Hammer Museum. Grinnan has been included in many group exhibitions, including the *2004 Whitney Biennial* at the Whitney Museum, *Real World: The Dissolving Space of Experience* at Modern Art Oxford, and *The Artist Museum* at MOCA in Los Angeles. Her work is included in collections at MOCA, the Hammer Museum, LACMA and the Virginia Museum, and she has been awarded a Guggenheim fellowship and a Pollock-Krasner grant. She lives and works in Los Angeles.

Mount Wilson Observatory (right)

The performance at Mount Wilson Observatory took place on June 23–24, 2012 and was part of the group show, KNOWLEDGES, curated by Christina Ondrus and Elleni Sclavenitis. Mount Wilson Observatory is where Edwin Hubble made the significant discovery that the universe was expanding. The Astrology Orchestra was performed around the 60-inch telescope, the same telescope where Harlow Shapley discovered that our solar system is not at the center of the galaxy and that our position in space is decentralized.[2]

Integratron (left)

On Saturday, November 17, 2012 from 4:30 to 6:00pm, the Astrology Orchestra was performed at the Integratron, presented by LAND (Los Angeles Nomadic Division). The Integratron is a site with a rich history and mythology as it was built by George Van Tassel, an aeronautical engineer who left his job at Howard Hughes to build the structure. He claims that aliens gave him the information to build the dome and that it functions as a quasi-time machine and cell rejuvenator. It is built over an aquifer covering a geomagnetic spike in the earth. The inside of the dome is made of wood, constructed without nails or screws, making it a perfect resonator.[3]

Katie Grinnan, Astrology Orchestra, Performance at the Mount Wilson Observatory as part of KNOWLEDGES, curated by Christina Ondrus and Elleni Sclavenitis, 2012 (Image by Robert Wedemeyer)

Katie Grinnan, Astrology Orchestra, Performance at the Venice Beach Biennial, curated by Ali Subotnick in conjunction with the Made in LA Hammer Biennial, 2012 (Image by Robert Wedemeyer)

Venice Beach Biennial

On July 14, 2012 at 6PM, the Astrology Orchestra was performed at Venice Beach as part of the Hammer Museum's Venice Beach Biennial curated by Ali Subotnick. The famed Venice boardwalk is home to many eclectic sites, scenes, and characters such as muscle beach, head shops, drum circles, raucous performances, and the Venice Beach art community comprised of local artists and vendors. In this context, the orchestra operated in a similar fashion to a drum circle, although the sounds are discordant. The sound of the waves, police helicopters, beach-goers, and bike bells all added to the cacophony.[4]

Endnotes

1 Katie Grinnan, *The Astrology Orchestra: A Project by Katie Grinnan* (Los Angeles: LAND [Los Angeles Nomadic Division], 2014), p. 6.

2 Grinnan, *The Astrology Orchestra*, p. 34.

3 Grinnan, *The Astrology Orchestra*, p. 42.

4 Grinnan, *The Astrology Orchestra*, p. 38.

(Above) Katie Grinnan, Instruments at the Venice Beach Biennial, 2012 (Image by Mikki Saito)

(Right) Katie Grinnan, Detail of Mars instrument at the Venice Beach Biennial, 2012 (Image by Collin Cook)

Katie Grinnan, Astrology Orchestra, Exhibition installation view at Human Resources, 2014; A LAND (Los Angeles Nomadic Division) Exhibition (Image courtesy of Jeff McLane)

Human Use *of* Radioactive Isotopes:
The Problem that *Won't Go Away*

by J. Lee LEHMAN, PHD

IT'S HARD TO BELIEVE that human use of radioactivity is just over one hundred years old. In 1896, Henri Becquerel began the study of it, shortly to be eclipsed by Marie Curie when she began her examinations later in the same year. It was from Curie that we have the name radioactivity.

It took several years for this early research to develop into anything industrially useful. The work of Marie and Pierre Curie led to interest in nuclear medicine, an ironic development, given the toxicity that would be recognized in the future from radioisotopes.[1] It would be the 1940s before the horrible military uses would be realized after the first successful nuclear chain reaction occurred, with this same breakthrough also opening the way for civilian nuclear power generation in 1951.

Advertisements at world's fairs in the 1950s and 1960s trumpeted the prediction that soon electrical power would be so cheap that it wouldn't even be metered, and right at the heart of these plans was nuclear power. Despite all the hype, virtually free electricity has not happened. Nuclear power accounts for about 11% of the electricity generated globally, with over one hundred nuclear plants in the USA alone. This original rosy picture for nuclear power has not been achieved because:

- There are absolutely no solutions to the "safe" disposal of waste which will remain dangerously radioactive for periods of up to 250,000 years or more.

- There is no way to prevent human errors which result in catastrophic failures of plants, with attendant release of radioactive materials into the environment.

- Material failures also occur, as well as weather or earthquake disasters.

- Nuclear power plants use at least 2–3 times more water than non-nuclear power plants.

In examining the many nuclear accidents in the past, three events stand out as first tier. These three events are the three times where there has been a severe meltdown at a nuclear power plant:

- Three Mile Island (Pennsylvania, 1979)
- Chernobyl (Ukraine, 1986)
- Fukushima (Japan, 2011)

Ultimately, we may wish to study these charts to address whether we expect the rest of the twenty-first century to include more catastrophic nuclear events. But first, there are two different approaches that we need to consider. The typical astrological approach to a disaster is to examine the chart of it to either make predictions about further events, or to justify what already happened. The more difficult approach is to ask whether mundane charts such as eclipses, ingresses, or conjunctions for the time period might show or predict anything about the disaster.

THREE MILE ISLAND

Let's first consider Three Mile Island. It was caused by a stuck valve which released coolant, compounded by operator error. Fortunately there were no immediate casualties; unfortunately there was no record of the extent to which radioactive gases like cesium were released. Epidemiology suggests that Three Mile Island contributed to the development of many fatal cases of cancer, but this cannot be specifically proved.[2]

In *Astrology of Sustainability* I reviewed the Aries Ingress for Washington which occurred just before Three Mile Island.[3] That was one of the rare cases where the Aries Ingress for Washington featured the Sun conjunct the IC. From 1700–2060, there are only four instances of this configuration with an orb of less than two degrees. This unusual configuration is not something to anticipate fondly when it comes to land issues: in the past, it was also the marker for the Dust Bowl in the 1930s. Its most recent occurrence corresponded to the devastation of Hurricane Sandy in 2012, an event with an environmental impact so vast it has not

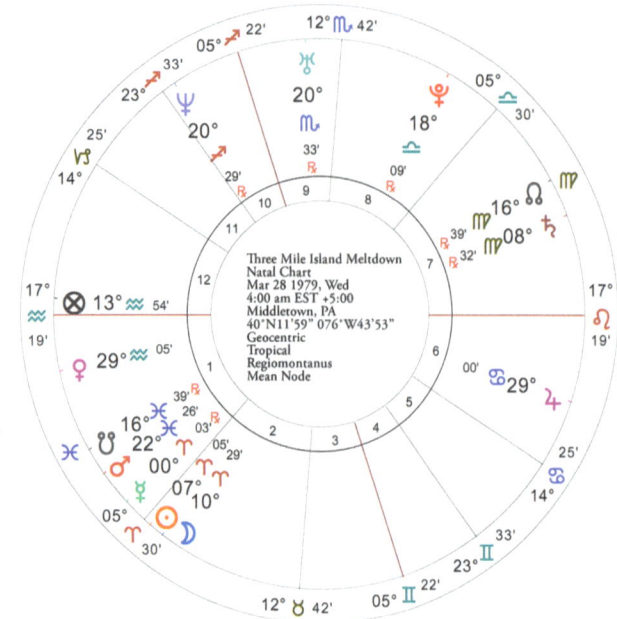

even begun to be understood.

So far, the Sun conjunct IC signature has brought serious and unanticipated environmental devastation. With the Dust Bowl, it's still impossible to comprehend the magnitude of the soil loss. With Three Mile Island, we were confronted with a radiation event in our own backyard, with medical consequences that belied the peaceful use of atomic power promised by the atomic scientists. With Hurricane Sandy, the devastating winds damaged buildings storing chemicals in and around large population centers, where no one had ever expected that breakage and flooding could create unthinkable toxic mixtures. Again, with few immediate fatalities, and thousands of mystery chemical exposures, the actual human cost of this disaster will never be known.

The Aries Ingress of 2045 will again feature the Sun conjunct the IC for Washington—with a slightly wider orb than the prior examples. This Ingress does suggest the possibility of severe issues, with a packed 4th house (the land, and thus by extension, the environment), and Saturn rising. The prevalence of Fire in this chart would literally suggest fires, wars, or prominent global warming at that time. But this does not necessarily suggest something related to radioactivity, as we have not yet established a signature.

So to summarize, we do have an Aries Ingress chart which suggests the possibility of environmental disaster in the year in which Three Mile Island occurred. But what of the Three Mile Island chart itself? The first thing we may note about the Ascendant is that it's fixed: this suggests either an event that will unfold over a long period of time, or, as is true with many accidents, reaction time will be slow. Saturn rules the Ascendant—the event itself. Saturn is peregrine, and in the 7th house of open enemies, or open danger. Stan Barker made an interesting observation about Virgo as showing those matters related to the "common man." This turns out to be intriguing from the standpoint that we can understand the human error component of the accident as being an error of an operator: not the higher-ups, but a single person reacting too slowly (Saturn again!) to unanticipated circumstances.[4] The accident occurred just after a New Moon in Aries, roughly opposite Pluto. Here, the Ruler of the 8th at the Ascendant in Saturn's sign and Pluto in the 8th is a poignant signature for delayed death from cancer.

Chernobyl

Consider our next meltdown, Chernobyl. This occurred in Ukraine, then part of the Soviet Union. Only Chernobyl and Fukushima (which we will discuss shortly) have been classified as category 7 (the highest category) on the International Nuclear Events Scale. Three Mile Island was classified as a 5. At Chernobyl, there were thirty-one immediate fatalities, and uncounted cases of cancer in the population.

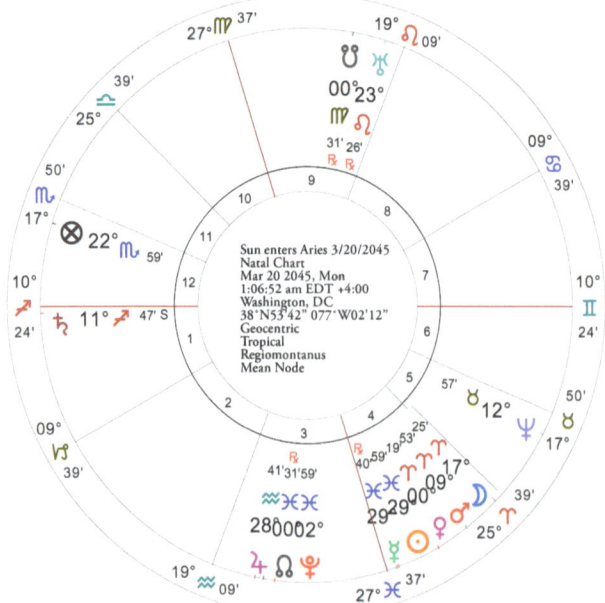

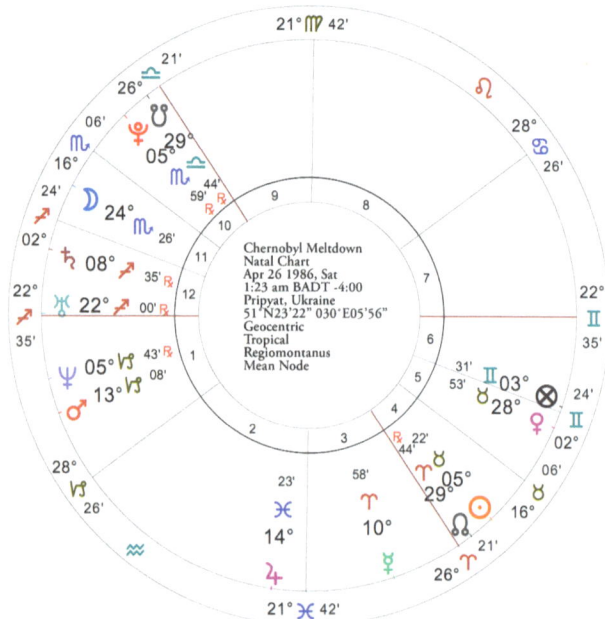

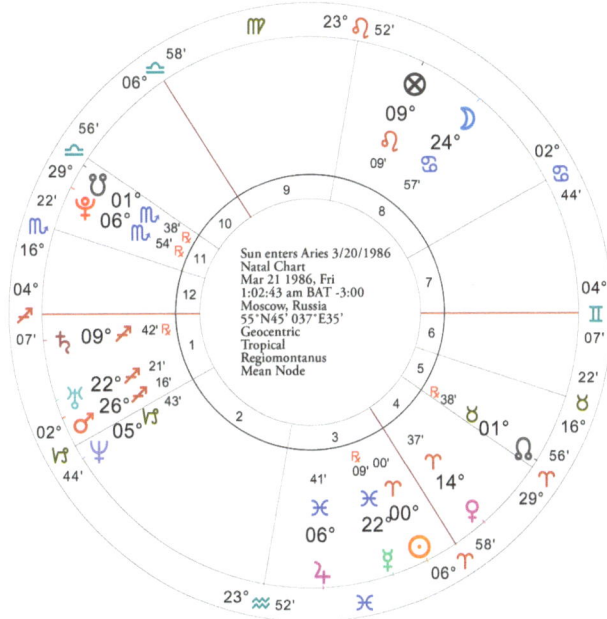
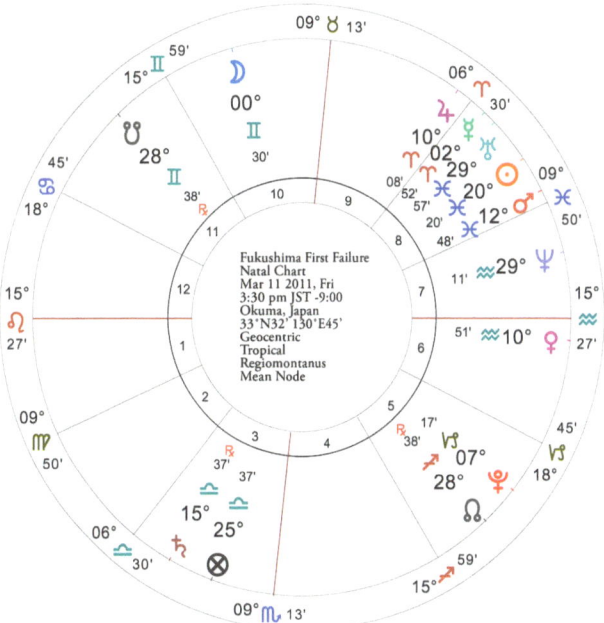

Scientists are still studying the region downwind for biological mutations. Clean-up involved half a million people. The cause was originally an unusual repair procedure on a blocked water filter, which inadvertently allowed water into an air line, cutting off cooling water to the reactor. An emergency state was tripped, stopping the chain reaction, but the reactor core still overheated in the absence of coolant.

The Aries Ingress for Moscow in 1986 shows the same pattern as the Ingress for Three Mile Island in the USA: the Sun near the IC. While not as exact as for Three Mile Island, Sagittarian Saturn, Uranus, and Mars in the 1st house are also suggestive of a major accident—the idea of meltdown is clearly present.

The chart for the time that the emergency state began looks so obvious we almost can't believe it: Uranus exactly rising for the time of the meltdown! Of course, Uranus (like every other planet) rises once a day anyway, but the partile Sun-Pluto opposition with Neptune in a partile sextile/trine configuration adds some punch. It also brings us to a question that we have not dealt with yet: what rules radioactivity? Many astrologers automatically assume that Pluto is the ruler of radioactivity, but I would express caution before automatically agreeing. Here, the Sun-Pluto opposition does support this idea.

Fukushima

The triggering event at Fukushima was a magnitude 9.0 earthquake. The actual failure occurred within three minutes of when a tsunami generated by that earthquake hit the complex. Unlike Three Mile Island and Chernobyl, where specific equipment failed and the operators did not know how to fix the problem, at Fukushima, four of the six reactors suffered widespread and critical failure of a non-specific nature. Within an hour of the earthquake, the entire complex—not just one reactor—had been inundated by seawater.

The earthquake-tsunami combination that devastated Fukushima was entirely predictable—after all, Japan is a series of volcanic islands frequently beset by major earthquakes. Amazingly, despite Fukushima being close to five different fault lines, the government continues to try to maintain the fiction that these plants are earthquake hardened.[5] Clearly, the government could not bring itself to consider the possibility that an offshore quake could trigger a tsunami? In other words, because the sequence which caused Fukushima *was* in fact conceivable, it *could* have been prevented with a more robust risk aversion policy by the Japanese government.

The Aries Ingress for Tokyo in the year in which Fukushima occurred had a Moon–Part of Fortune partile opposition square Neptune. This not only foreshadows the event, but also the high cost of cleanup, and the damage to the ocean. This configuration could be read this way:

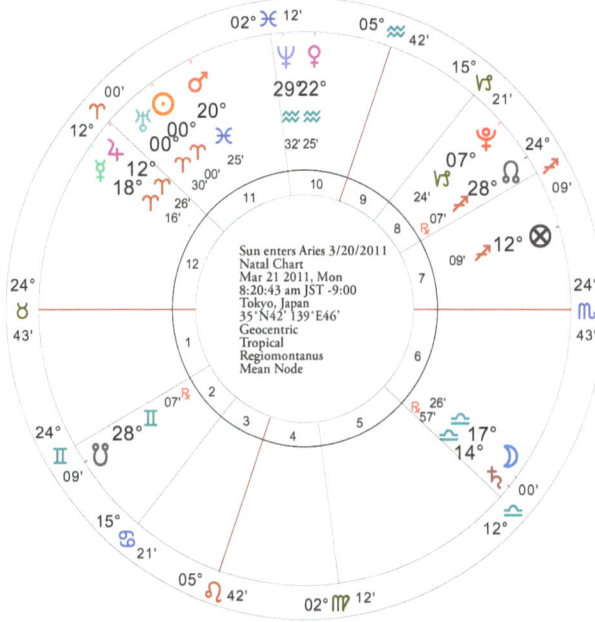

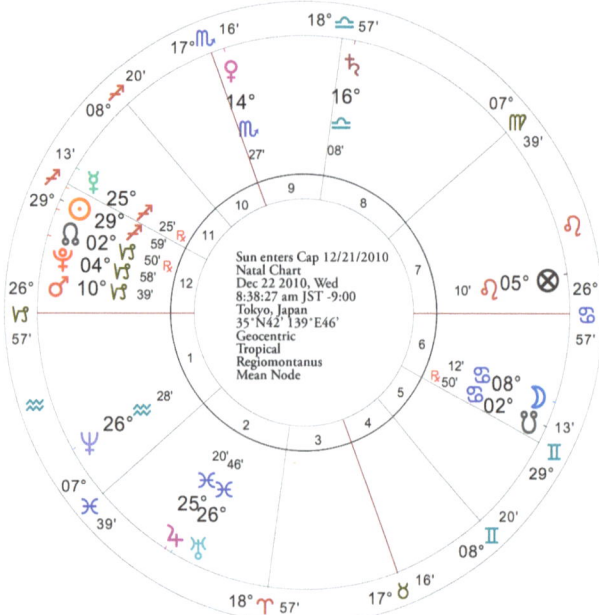

beware of events relating to the sea! The event itself fell rather late in the year, and because the angles of the Aries Ingress were cardinal, according to traditional method it was necessary to use all four cardinal ingresses for interpretation. The dramatic Capricorn Ingress for 2010 fell just prior to the event. The Ingress itself occurred just hours after a lunar eclipse. In Tokyo the degree of that eclipse fell at the 12th house cusp, thereby suggesting events outside the conscious control of the normal cast of characters: dare we say, self-undoing? The Sun, North Node, Pluto, and Mars all fall within a ten-degree span in the 12th house. A Jupiter-Uranus conjunction occurs in the 2nd, reiterating the financial issue we saw already in the Aries Ingress chart. The prominence of the 12th–6th axis, with the Moon in the 6th is ominous, because the problem with Fukushima was not the fatalities that occurred that day, but the massive and continued release of poisonous radioactivity into the Pacific Ocean and land environment that will continue to occur for years, if not decades.

I am discussing this because Fukushima presents us with an entirely different scenario than Three Mile Island and Chernobyl. The earlier two meltdowns had two important things in common:

¶ The primary effect was at least initially land-based, and so our 4th house model makes a lot of sense

¶ They occurred as a result of material failure and human error

Fukushima was, by contrast, an act of nature. Prediction of such events presumably involves different parameters. Earthquakes, however, traditionally fall under astrometeorology. While astrometeorology has been a topic in astrology for millennia, what I would point out is that it developed under the assumption that the weather is a process of the Earth, and thus on a different scale and magnitude than events that directly involve human souls. I want to dodge for the moment any issue of human involvement in climate change simply to point out that we have to operate our predictive models according to the nature of the events that we wish to predict. If extreme weather can cause an effect, then it may be the weather we need to predict, not the effect. The Mercury square Jupiter-Uranus in the Capricorn Ingress prior to Fukushima could well be a harbinger of a storm, but now we also enter the realm of earthquake weather, which is itself a vexed subject, both astrologically and otherwise.

In examining the chart for Fukushima, we are not *predicting* the event, but showing its aftermath. Here we see the Sun ruling the Ascendant in the 8th house of death, accompanied by Mars, Uranus, and Mercury. That the bulk of these are in water signs perhaps is suggestive of the literally oceanic effects of this accident, but also this may relate to the fact that these were water-cooled reactors, one of the most unstable design types. The continued release of contaminated cooling water is one of the devastating effects of this disaster. This was the last gasp of Uranus in Pisces, conjunct the fixed star Scheat, one of the baleful fixed stars, and with Uranus also at the Bendings, the points square the Nodes. The Moon at zero degrees shows the action is just beginning, and that much needs to be done. The link it provides between being in the 10th and ruling the 12th shows that decisions by higher-ups will continue to be crucial in solving the problem, but that the first tendency of these higher-ups will be to sweep these problems under the 12th-house rug.

Peregrine Venus ruling the 10th shows the absence of a clear of strategy by the CEO of TEPCO, the power company. The Moon in the 10th cries out for action by the Chief Executive, but the Moon is likewise peregrine, which shows what we have seen since the accident: incompetence, vacillation, misinformation, cover-up, and a complete vacuum of leadership, which they act out in the random walk that is so diagnostic of the peregrine condition. That they have no comprehensive plan is painfully obvious.

A Model for Meltdowns?

We have seen that the cause of the meltdown may be important in determining its astrology. As we have seen, there is much more in common in the lead-up to both Three Mile Island and Chernobyl, which had similar causes, than either of those to Fukushima. We have identified one time in the future for the USA—2045—that matches our existing tentative model. But of course, every Aries Ingress will have the Sun conjunct the IC *somewhere* on the globe, so this is not yet a completely satisfactory nor complete prediction.

What about Radioactivity in General?

Astrologers in the past have mostly studied nuclear energy as it was used in the atomic bomb. In this regard, Troinski's 1956 book was of major importance, and one of the works that established Pluto as the ruler of radioactivity.[6] In the sense that nuclear reactions are literally the transformation of one element into another, this does match well with Pluto as ruler of transformation. The question is: can we make meaningful correlations with charts related to radioactivity in general? At least with respect to the atomic bomb, I'm not sure we can.

When we consider the charts themselves for key moments in the development of the atomic bomb, we do find a certain prominence to Pluto, but not so much so that it is overwhelming:

¶ For the first nuclear chain reaction (the root chart for both nuclear power plants and the atomic bomb in the USA), Pluto is angular, but so is the Saturn-Uranus conjunction, and the Sun, Mercury, and Venus.

¶ In the case of the first atomic explosion (the test for the deployment of the atomic bomb), Pluto, the Sun and the Moon were angular. The Sun and the Moon are angular according to the five degree rule, where angularity is defined as extending five degrees onto the cadent side of an angle, which is the normal Medieval definition. In fact, according to the Medieval definition, both the Sun and the Moon are stronger than Pluto, because it was the angle itself (or any other house cusp) which was considered to be the strongest manifestation of the energy of the house.

¶ For the destruction of Hiroshima, Pluto was combust and succedent, while Uranus was partile conjunct the MC.

¶ In the case of the bombing of Nagasaki, Pluto was in the 10th and still combust.

I do have to admit that the symbolism of a Sun-Pluto conjunction for the dropping of the two atomic bombs is a hugely satisfying symbolism, if the word satisfying can even be applied to two such horrific events—but this would be true whether Pluto is really taken as the ruler of radioactivity or not.

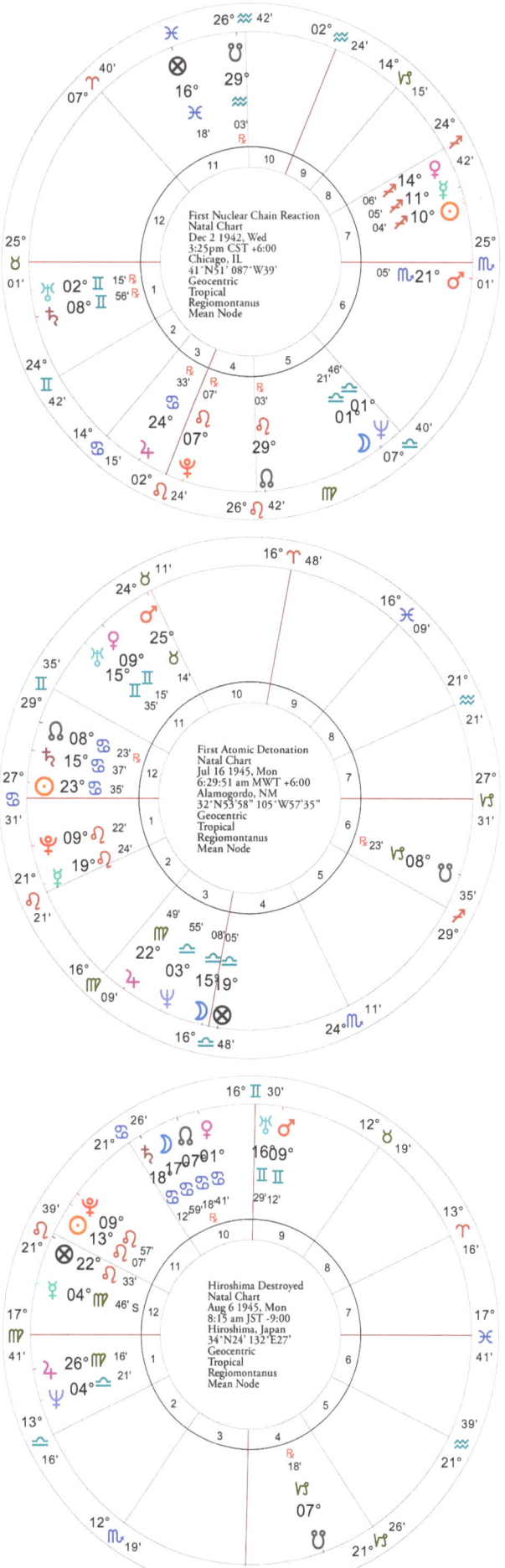

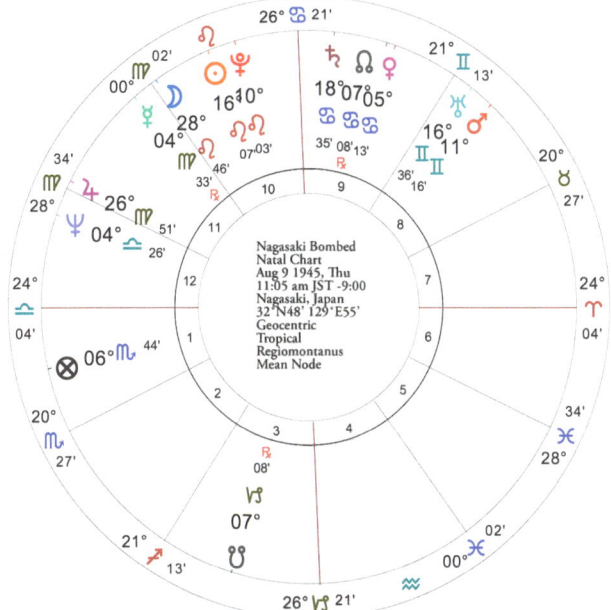

59

Pluto was prominent in the Aries Ingress of 1945 prior to the testing and dropping of the two bombs—but in the chart calculated for Tokyo, not Washington. In Tokyo, Pluto was conjunct the IC, highlighting the plight of the victims of the bomb, but not telling the story of the perpetrators in Washington. And this is the cause for concern: the action was coming from Washington, not Tokyo.

Let's examine one more Aries Ingress with respect to radioactivity: the Ingress of 1939, calculated for Washington. Most of the time, we see the 1939 Aries Ingress presented for Berlin or London, because the emphasis is on the outbreak of World War II in that year. Again, as I discussed in *Astrology of Sustainability*, the beginning of World War II seems correlated with the ingress of Pluto into Leo, just as Pluto's ingress into Cancer seemed to signal the beginning of World War I. But Washington is generally skipped for 1939, because the USA did not enter the war until much later. However, it is well known that Franklin Roosevelt was sympathetic to the Allied cause, and was much more ready to get involved than the average American citizen understood at the time.

But I digress. In 1939, a number of European physicists who were residing in the USA realized that the implications of the discovery of nuclear fission by Otto Hahn and Fritz Strassmann in 1938 included the possibility of the production of an atomic bomb. They reasoned that its destructive potential was enormous, orders of magnitude larger than conventional armaments, thus making its possessor militarily invincible. Believing that the Nazis would develop this weapon, they felt that it was vital for the USA to develop this technology first, or at least simultaneously. To this end, Leo Szilárd teamed up with several of his colleagues to write a letter to Roosevelt signed by Albert Einstein, as the most prominent of their number. This letter was given to Roosevelt in a briefing on 11 October 1939. Roosevelt replied to Einstein, and began to set in motion the wheels that would eventually result in the Manhattan Project.

The Aries Ingress for 1939 was the last hurrah for Pluto in Cancer: we see it here at 29 degrees, in a partile square to the Ascendant at Washington. Mars too was in a partile square to the Sun from the 9th. We *would* become involved in a foreign war. But the last degree of the Ascendant reveals the plot: the USA was still enmeshed in its isolationism, although the dreams of conquest were already there. The leader (Roosevelt), given by Saturn, ruler of the 10th, was in Detriment—not a powerful position, but with its 12th house placement, he was already working behind the scenes to change the pacifistic inclinations of the majority of Americans.

Remember that in a year with a cardinal sign on the angle for an Aries Ingress, all four cardinal ingresses are necessary to read the year. So for the October meeting with Roosevelt, the Libra Ingress is used. By this time, Pluto had moved into Leo as surely as Germany had moved into Czechoslovakia, and one of the things that Germany gained by that invasion was access to uranium mines. We see the two classical malefics in a partile square, and thus also square/opposite the Aries Ingress Pluto position. The 10th house ruler Jupiter was in bellicose Aries, and the Moon was only two degrees from the degree of Roosevelt's Sun: he had watched in dismay as isolationism kept the USA out of World War I for years. Einstein's letter, while not specifically predicted by this ingress chart, would definitely fall upon receptive ears.

While Pluto might seem less compelling for being succedent, we do note that it was at the Bendings, and also not far from the opposition to the Moon, which itself keyed into Roosevelt's natal chart. Roosevelt's own solar return for 1939 had Pluto in Leo: it had retrograded back to Cancer before the Aries Ingress. Roosevelt had already passed into the new paradigm. As I noted in *Classical Solar Returns*,

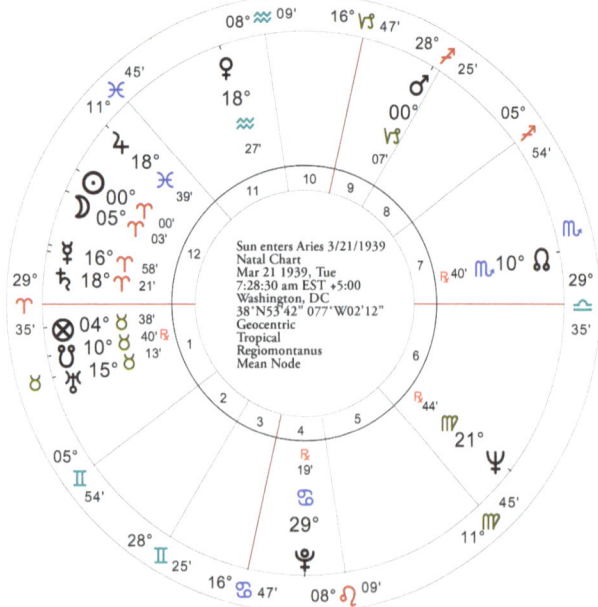
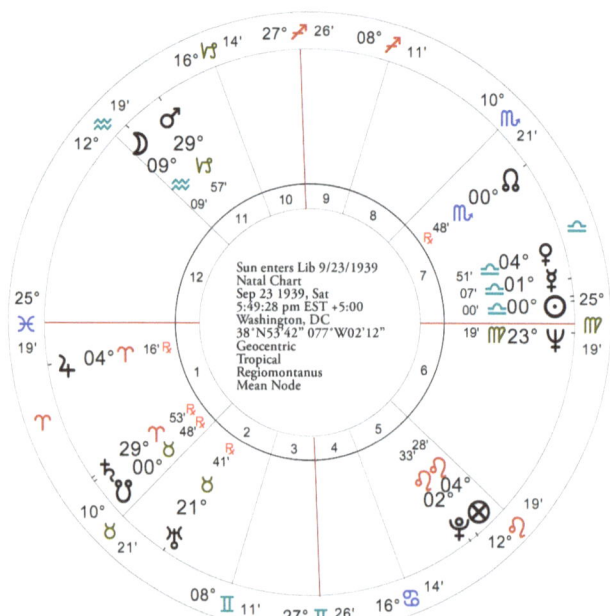

during this period of time, Roosevelt's solar returns were "leading" the Aries Ingresses: he was getting configurations a year before the USA was.[7] By being ahead of the curve, he could anticipate and plan for coming events.

Fixed Stars

But if the Aries Ingresses have a strong Pluto story, at least for the development of nuclear energy as a weapon, what then can we say for the charts of the events themselves? One thing we can note is the frequency of the most common fixed stars, which we shall limit to the Royal Stars and the short list of baleful stars. Consider:

- The first nuclear chain reaction occurred with Saturn at Aldebaran, the North Node at Regulus, and Algol rising.
- The first atomic explosion occurred with Venus conjunct Aldebaran, Mars conjunct Algol, and the South Node conjunct Facies.
- For the destruction of Hiroshima, Mars had moved on to Aldebaran.
- For Nagasaki, the Moon was conjunct Regulus.

The frequency of Aldebaran is interesting. The star itself is the eye of the bull of Taurus, one of the four Royal Stars. Diana K. Rosenberg discussed how the anatomical location of a star is important in its interpretation, and she also discussed how blindness stars like Aldebaran apply to both blindness and acute vision.[8] I think here the story line is how the single-pointed desire to develop a weapon was pursued without any consideration about consequences—and that in itself is a form of hubris, the great subtext of the Royal Stars. Dennis Wainstock documented as well the complete determination of American politicians to actually use the bomb, despite indications that the war against Japan could have been ended earlier—and with fewer US, not to mention Japanese, casualties.[9]

Facies was a star that was conjunct Hitler's natal Moon, so its presence here may directly relate to the development of the bomb based upon fear that Hitler would do so first.

If the fixed stars are especially strong during the military development, did this carry over to civilian accidents? It appears that it may. For our three meltdowns:

- At Three Mile Island, Mercury was conjunct Scheat, a top rank malefic star, while the IC was conjunct Aldebaran, and the MC Antares. Antares (the heart of the Scorpion) and Aldebaran are opposite each other in ecliptic longitude, and thus often linked together in patterns.
- At the time of Chernobyl, Saturn was at Antares, and thus opposite its position for the first nuclear chain reaction.
- For Fukushima, Uranus was conjunct Scheat, and the Moon was conjunct Alcyone.

Notice the absence of Royal Stars for Fukushima, although the catastrophe stars are there. This is a small sample, but could this be the absence of an immediate human cause?

Here, the appearance of fixed stars of an appropriate nature seems more obvious as a marker than Pluto, although Uranus certainly is evident. But the presence of Uranus may show once again its sudden disruptive nature rather than anything specifically related to nuclear energy.

> I am *not* so convinced that Pluto is the ONLY RULER for *radioactivity*.

So what is the Ruler of Radioactivity?

Based on these charts, I am not so convinced that Pluto is the only ruler for radioactivity. I have found that oftentimes new discoveries may not point so much to the outer planets as the possibility of multiple and possibly interactive rulerships. In fact, when we examine the historical basis for rulership, we may conclude that rulerships have seldom been on a one-to-one basis anyway. If we accept this premise, then we can turn the question around, and ask what properties of nuclear energy are most like which particular planets:

- Pluto may rule the actual chemistry or physics of radioactive decay itself, because this is true alchemy as it was originally defined: the transmutation of one element into another.
- Saturn would have two things to contribute. Saturn is the traditional ruler of poisons, and radioactivity is very toxic. The second is the longevity of the storage problem of radioactive waste, because there is a long time component when these substances retain their toxic biological properties.
- The Sun has been repeatedly used as a symbol for atomic explosions. In popular literature, it is described as a ball of fire, and that's besides Simon and Garfunkel's "The Sun is Burning," about a nuclear detonation. Here we see especially an indicator for an interactive Sun-Pluto signature.

While one should be cautious about pushing metaphors too far, the fact that the one example we have of spontaneous alchemy produces such a dangerous effect for living creatures is perhaps an incredible warning about alchemy approached glibly, casually, or unconsciously. Left to their own devices, these processes can blow up, and are dangerous for humans.

This also supports my general contention that many astrologers have ignored the lessons that the outer planets signify. They are the realm of the chthonic entities, those processes of fate which are so large and so remote that a mere human life is but a grain of sand when they impinge upon our lives. An individual citizen of Hiroshima could do nothing to save him or herself on 6 August 1945. These processes ultimately make a mockery of our normal beliefs about power and control. While we may from time to time intuit eddies and currents with their realm, their scale of existence is so vast compared to ours that we can never truly understand or control them. It is to this scale that the energy of the atom belongs.

"Virgo," by Larkin Cypher, for the Constellation art show

Endnotes

1 As one of the truly fascinating studies of the shadow side of the development of a technology, the great pioneer in radiation biology, John Gofman, established that there is no threshold below which radioactivity ceases to be dangerous to biological entities. Nonetheless, medicine has been unable to resist the penetrating power of radioactive analysis, putting medicine in the awkward position of using a poison to diagnose disease conditions. See: John W. Gofman, *Radiation and Human Health* (New York: Pantheon Books, 1983).

2 M. C. Hatch, S. Wallenstein, J. Beyea, & M. Susser, 'Cancer rates after the Three Mile Island nuclear accident and proximity of residence to the plant,' *Americal Journal of Public Health* 81, no. 6 (June, 1991): pp. 719–24; S. Wing, D.B. Richardson, & W. Hoffmann, 'Cancer Risks near Nuclear Facilities: The Importance of Research Design and Explicit Study Hypotheses,' *Environmental Health Perspectives* 119, no. 4 (Apr 2011): pp. 417–21.

3 J. Lee Lehman, J. Lee, *Astrology of Sustainability: The Challenge of Pluto in Capricorn* (Atglen, PA: Schiffer Press, 2011), pp. 142–49.

4 Stan Barker, *The Signs of the Times : The Neptune Factor and America's Destiny* (St. Paul, MN: Llewellyn Publications, 1984), p. 160.

5 See, for example, http://www.tokyotimes.com/Utilities-research-finds-14-fault-lines-near-Japan-s-nuclear-plants/

6 E. H. Troinski, Das Horoskop Des Atom-Zeitalters (Hannover: Baumgartner-Verlag, 1956).

7 J. Lee Lehman, *Classical Solar Returns* (Atglen, PA: Schiffer Press, 2012), p. 314.

8 Diana K. Rosenberg, *Secrets of the Ancient Skies*, 2 vols. (Ancient Skies Press, 2012).

9 Dennis Wainstock, *The Decision to Drop the Atomic Bomb* (Westport, CT: Praeger, 1996).

J. Lee Lehman has a Ph.D. in Botany from Rutgers University. She is Vice President of the Board of OCA Corp., and she teaches at IAA, the Midwest School of Astrology, and Kepler College. Dr. Lehman was a Professor and Vice President for Academic Affairs at Kepler College during its degree-granting phase. She is author of many books, including *Essential Dignities* (1989), *The Book of Rulerships* (1992), *The Martial Art of Horary Astrology* (2002), and *Classical Solar Returns* (2012). She served the astrological community as Research Director for NCGR from 1987-99, as UAC Board Treasurer from 1990-99, and as UAC Program Chair for UACs 1995 and 1998. Dr. Lehman is also the recipient of the 1995 Marc Edmund Jones Award and the 2008 Regulus Award for Education.

"Unveiling Gemini," by Benjamin Vierling, for the Constellation art show

"The Jester holds the dualistic personae of comedy and tragedy in his wry hands. Under the idiot's crested cowl is the glittering cosmic face of the infinite; the inquisitive mind that is the signature attribute of Gemini. Alternating masks invert established paradigms in order to discover oblique truths, embodying the maxim, *Nichts ist wahr, Alles ist erlaubt.* On the Jester's motley shoulder perches a bi-toned Magpie, trickster and collector of mischief par excellence."

Just as the Internet and mobile computing have changed every aspect of society over the course of the last twenty years, Virtual Reality is poised to have a similarly pervasive effect on our lives. The types of visceral experiences that VR can provide are truly unique, and on the whole constitute a new communications medium that will amount to the Gutenberg Press of the twenty-first century. Felt experiences will be able to be captured and shared just as books were able to capture and share information and knowledge. Just as new insights into perspective catalyzed breakthroughs in Renaissance art, then adding a new immersive dimension to computing will likely spur a similar revolutionary change in what types of experiences that can be shared through

There have been 3D environments in computer games since the early 80s, and interactive virtual worlds like Second Life since 2003. While immersive virtual reality includes some components of virtual environments, it also provides other elements that are completely new and different that transcend what is possible through a 2D medium.

Sébastien Kuntz defines Immersive Virtual Reality as "the science and technology required for a user to feel present, via perceptive, cognitive and functional immersion and interaction in a computer-generated environment."[1] There is a sense that you are transported into another world where the unconscious parts of your perception are fooled into believing that the computer-generated reality is actually

interactions like head tracking where your physical movements are mirrored within a virtual 3D environment to the point that they match your expectations. Even though your rational mind may realize that you are not in another world, your unconscious perceptions and primitive limbic mind will react as if the environment was real.

The second component of plausibility is when your cognition is fooled. As Kuntz says, "Everything that happens is coherent. You actually believe you are there, your actions have a credible impact on the virtual environment and your sensations are affected by it."[3] Attaining a sense of "presence" is the ultimate goal of a VR experience, but there is no fixed set of ingredients that reliably produce it. What is known is that there are a combination of components

The *Future of* Immersive Astrology

by Kent Bye

virtual reality. As such, the influence that virtual reality will have on astrology will be multi-faceted and profound, and could open up a new branch of astrology that I have been calling "Immersive Astrology." In order to investigate what types of new interactions that VR will be able to provide to astrologers, then it would be helpful to first dive into the key components of what constitutes "virtual reality."

What is Immersive Virtual Reality?

There is a large difference between 3D virtual worlds that are experienced through a 2D screen, and a completely immersive virtual reality experience.

real. Within the VR community, this is widely referred to as the experience of "presence."

VR researcher Mel Slater defines two key components that are necessary for people to have a realistic response to a virtual reality environment. He says, "The first is 'being there', often called 'presence', the qualia of having a sensation of being in a real place. We call this Place Illusion (PI). Second, Plausibility Illusion (Psi) refers to the illusion that the scenario being depicted is actually occurring... when both PI and Psi occur, participants will respond realistically to the virtual reality."[2]

Some of the elements that trick your perception into believing that you are in another place are real-time

that together constitute "virtual reality," but taken individually are merely a part of a virtual world.

Some of these components are if a participant is able to see real-time, computer-generated, 3D environments that provide a sense of depth perception through a stereoscopic display and low-latency head tracking. Having 3D sound that reacts to head movements is also a key aspect to creating immersion. Being able to have natural interactions within the virtual environment that are similar to how you would do the same action in the real world also helps make the scenario believable. Being able to see your body, and have your limbs be tracked is a key aspect of tricking your mind that what you are seeing is real. Doing physical actions like walking or running on an omnidirectional treadmill can activate a powerful component of our unconscious minds that provide a sense of immersion. Finally, one of the most powerful yet most difficult components of creating immersion in VR are haptics. These are technologies that provide force reactions to virtual objects to simulate our sense of touch.

We are at the very beginnings of what is possible for Immersive Astrology, and so I'll be making some predictions of what might be cool astrological experiences to have within VR. It is important to note that until these ideas are actually implemented within VR, then they are just hypotheses or speculations. Sometimes something that you imagine would be really awesome in VR actually ends up being pretty terrible because it either causes motion sickness, is too intense, or just feels uncomfortable to the participant. Not only that, but each person reacts differently and has different thresholds for what they can comfortably handle in VR.

Virtual Reality is a new communications medium that is still in a "Wild West" phase where many possibilities are being explored through short, experimental experiences. There are also no standard conventions yet for how to work with this new medium. There is a lot of innovation happening with VR right now, and it is very likely that the most compelling aspects of Immersive Astrology will be things that we cannot even imagine at this stage of VR's evolution.

I'll be providing my best predictions for what is possible in Immersive Astrology based upon evidence and findings from these early experiments, as well as from Oculus VR's own best practices guide for what does and does not work in VR.[4]

Stepping into your Chart

One of the first and most obvious applications of Immersive Astrology will be to provide an opportunity to step into your natal chart and experience it from a first-person perspective. There are a number of diverse, immersive vantage points that I think would be compelling and could potentially provide new ways for tuning into the relationships between planets within a chart.

Our minds have evolved to have an amazing ability to remember locations and spatial relationships, and virtual reality has the potential to tap into and leverage the power of our spatial memory.

Imagine that you are standing in the center of your chart within a circular room that is split into twelve signs and houses where the ecliptic is parallel to the floor. Each of your natal chart planets are positioned at a fixed distance against the wall located at its

"Aquarius," photography by Michael S. Williams, for the Constellation *art show*

proper longitude, but also at its correct latitude.

Each planet could be represented by a planetary sphere that is textured to mimic what each planet physically looks like. Alternatively, the planets could be represented by their glyph or a combination of glyph and sphere. There may be slight differences in scale between the planets, but it is not likely at the correct relative scale because the important information is the longitude and latitude information for the intent of astrological delineation.

Standing in the center of your chart and being able to look all around could be insightful, but I think the really compelling perspective would be to step into a planet's position in order to see what other planets are in aspect to it. This would be similar to the practice of Astro Drama where you stand in the shoes of a planet and then connect and communicate to other planets that make a Ptolemaic aspect. There could be aspect lines that could be toggled on and off to help see these spatial relationships between the planets.

There is also the potential to tap into the lessons from the practice of family constellation work, which also relies upon placing characters within a 3D space and then tuning into how their relative positions reflect the dynamic of their relationship. Immersive Astrology has the potential to use similar techniques, especially when it comes to looking at transits and how the relationship dynamic changes as the aspects between them change.

The next immersive perspective could be the full geocentric perspective where the ecliptic has its proper orientation, and you are able to see the position of each planet relative to the fixed stars, constellations and horizon line. You'll be able to see what the sky looked like when you were born, and you could turn on overlays of the constellation drawings that connect the dots between the stars. If you were born during the day, then you should also be able to toggle off the effect of the sun in order to more quickly locate all of the planetary positions.

The relative magnitude could also be implemented to help distinguish planets from stars, as well as a hovering display panel for unobtrusively showing additional information either within the main field of view or down by your side. It is important to have these types of display options be able to be toggled on and off in order to increase the immersion and sense of presence. People may want to just soak in the night sky without having a lot of synthetic text killing the vibe.

There would also likely need to be a number of 3D symbolic translations in order to maximize the astrological value of the data. A simple example would be to include the outer planetary positions relative to the other fixed stars even though technically we wouldn't be able to see them with our naked eyes.

The 2D natal chart is an amazingly effective symbolic translation of the planetary positions that are located in 3D space and time. There is a lot of astronomical information and details that are lost within this compression, but it is a tradeoff that we make in order to render the process of astrological delineation more efficient. I imagine that there will need to be some similar symbolic translations performed within virtual reality in order to maximize the use of the medium. Sometimes literal accuracy will need to be sacrificed in order to either make a more comfortable VR experience, or to make the astrological insights more effective.

For example, one symbolic translation that needs to be figured out is how to depict the planets that are located in the first to sixth houses within a geocentric perspective. These are technically blocked from view due to the earth being in the way, and so there are a number of different options for representing these planets.

The option where the ecliptic is parallel to the horizon would be one simple way to solve this, but then you would lose the actual appearance of the night sky relative to the horizon line.

Another translation option would be to make the earth a translucent material that would reveal any planets located in the lower quadrants. The problem with this solution is that the initial virtual reality experiences are designed to be sit-down experiences, and so it is not going to be comfortable to ask people to turn around 180 degrees in their chair in addition to having to look down at an angle in order to see the contents of their first to sixth houses.

One technical solution would be to multiply the amount that you turn in VR relative to how much you are actually turning. For example, turning 120 degrees from facing forward in real life could be multiplied and translated into a full 180-degree turn within VR. The visual field dominates perception, and so the user may not even realize this offset as evidenced by a technique called "redirected walking" that allows infinite locomotion within a finite space.[5]

Another solution could be to mirror the first to sixth houses to be straight in front of you and below a translucent horizon. You could also try to rotate your avatar from looking south to looking north to be able to look down at the first to sixth houses. Or you could artificially lock the planetary positions and diurnally rotate the earth so that the first to sixth houses were located in the seventh to twelfth houses. Or similarly, you could transport yourself to the other side of the earth and see what the sky looked like at that precise moment. This approach would be an imprecise representation of which houses these planets were located in, but if you are interested in seeing the connection of planets to the fixed stars then this could be a viable approach.

A final perspective that could be interesting in VR would be the heliocentric perspective. Imagine having a miniature Orrery model at your feet where you could look directly down at the sun and see all of the planets rotating around it. It would be easy to start to correlate how close planets are to each other, and understand the mechanics behind the fluctuations in magnitude over the course of a synodic cycle.

Before moving on to other potentials for immersive astrology, it is worth mentioning how VR could impact how you experience and work with your existing 2D astrological toolkit.

Ultimate Expansion of Screen Real Estate

The existing 2D natal chart is not going away any time soon, and virtual reality has the potential to make chart delineation more efficient. Bloomberg has been investigating how VR can revolutionize data analysis by displaying the equivalent of 10-40 computer screens at the same time.[6] Imagine entering in a birth date and immediately having access to dozens of views and techniques at your fingertips.

Not only would you have quick access to all of your existing astrological techniques from your toolkit, but there will be new types of data visualization techniques that fully take advantage of the expanded screen real estate and extra dimension for displaying data.

One example would be a three-dimensional, 90-degree graphical ephemeris, which typically compresses onto one plane all of the cardinal signs from 0-30 degrees, the fixed signs from 30-60 and the mutable signs from 60-90. It would be possible in VR to portray four slices of depth for a 90-degree ephemeris so that it would be easier to tell whether an aspect was a conjunction, square or opposition based upon which depth layer the transiting and natal planets occupied.

Reclaiming the Night Sky

Another potent application of Immersive Astrology is the ability to show an unobstructed view of the night sky. As was pointed out in the documentary *The City Dark*, over two thirds of the world's population live in urban areas that suffer from some form of light pollution.[7]

Imagine putting on a virtual reality head-mounted display, and then looking up to see the entire night sky in its full glory within your own personal planetarium. You would be able to see all of the stars as represented in that very moment, or go back to your moment of birth to see how your planets fit into the story of the constellations using Bernadette Brady's Visual Astrology techniques.

There could be overlays that would help you learn which stars constitute the twelve zodiacal constellations. And being able to adjust the magnitude threshold for which stars are displayed would allow you to mimic the night sky for where you live or being able to reveal all of the stars with a full and clear view of the Milky Way galaxy.

There are a number of ancient techniques of looking at the brightness of the star at specific moments, as well as tracking a planet through its various stages of synodic cycles. Being able see an accurate representation of where the planets actually are located in the sky could allow us a way to start to tune into these types of archetypal visual energies in a more potent way.

This leads into illustrating elements of celestial mechanics in a way that makes it easy to understand once you have seen it, but trying to understand it through descriptions alone doesn't really do it justice.

Celestial Mechanics

Through evolution, our eyes have a certain threshold for detecting motion. If change happens too slowly, then we cannot perceive it unless we accelerate time. Being within immersive virtual reality environments allows us to speed up time to the point where it reveals all of the changes in the sky that are too slow to see.

This would be the equivalent of taking some mesmerizing time lapse photography of the diurnal rotation of the night sky and then being able to dynamically experience that in real-time within a fully immersive world. In essence, virtual reality has the power to put you inside of a planetarium where you can experience your wildest astrological desires.

You could start to speed up time so that you could watch the diurnal rotation throughout the course of an entire day or week. You could then freeze the rotation of the earth so that the stars were fixed in one place, and then animate time so that you could watch how the planets move through the sky.

People might be surprised to learn that the planets are moving in the opposite direction than how the sun rises in the east and sets in the west. You could also animate the planet in three full dimensions, and not just in longitude and latitude, but also include distance in order to fully appreciate the full scope of retrograde movements.

There are other basic astronomical principles that are well suited for display in fully immersive environments. For example, showing the course of the sun throughout the day on the equinoxes as well as the summer and winter solstice in order to depict the difference of where the sun rises and sets at these extreme and balanced points, as well as how high in the sky the sun travels on each of these days.

You could also choose to animate the position of where the sun is located at high noon every day for a year in order to the show the analemma, the figure eight pattern that it makes.

Another time-lapse view that could be mesmerizing would be to, over the course of four to five minutes, watch the precession of the equinoxes over a full 26,000-year cycle as the north celestial pole moves in a full circle and the north star changes. Then watch how the vernal equinox precesses through the twelve signs of the zodiac over that long cycle.

A lot of these types of celestial mechanics are not strictly astrological, but it definitely helps ground astrologers into the astronomical foundations and knowing the basics of how the planets move through the heavens.

These types of astronomical celestial mechanics also have the potential to bring people into an immersive astrological experience even if they are not a believer or fan of astrology. They are the same types of basic mechanics that a professional planetarium at a museum would be teaching. VR has the power to not only bring these lessons into your home, but also to be able to add a distinct astrological flavor to them.

Scale

The *Titans of Space* VR experience takes you through a guided tour of our solar system, and it received very positive reactions from dozens of astrologers that I showed it to at the Northwest Astrological Conference in May of 2014.

One of the most impressive aspects of this demo is that it conveys the sense of relative scale between each of the planets. Being able to demonstrate scale is something that virtual reality really exceeds at, and so it makes sense to incorporate this within an Immersive Astrology program. There are no direct astrological insights that come from this, other than being able to provide the feeling of coming face-to-face with a planetary archetype.

Scale is also a way to start to experiment with demonstrating the Hermetic principle of *As above, So below*. For example, I could imagine being able to look into a mirror and seeing your avatar, but have it rendered as the Astrological Man distribution for how the signs correspond to different parts of the body. This would be a nice way to connect the microcosm of the planetary energies within your body with how the planets are arranged within the macrocosm.

Houses as Physical Rooms Decorated by Sign with Planetary Characters

One of the most exciting potentials for Immersive Astrology is that it could provide a non-verbal, archetypal experience that reflects someone's natal chart, or it could give a symbolic representation of transiting planetary energies that are happening at that very moment, from the past, or into the future.

What if you were to design a room or space for a specific house? How would the sign flavor the design of the room? And if a planet is in that sign, how would you design it as a character that reflects how it acts and behaves within that sign?

Imagine being able to take a virtual tour of each of your twelve houses where they are populated with virtual objects, art, and other integrated multi-media like YouTube videos or streaming music. What if the middle of your chart was portrayed as a type of medieval village with the planetary characters walking around and interacting with each other in a way that reflects their aspects? Squares and oppositions would be acting out that tension in some way, the trines and sextiles performing supportive actions, and characters with non-Ptolemeic aspects having trouble communicating with each other.

Michael Meade says that stories are spiritual acupuncture in that the details that stand out the most are usually connected your evolutionary edge and soul issues that you are working through at that moment.

Imagine if artificial intelligence gets good enough to be able carry out conversations and interactions that help you understand portions of your inner self. Or could it be possible to have a multi-threaded narrative story that plays out in parallel where you would be able to watch your transits unfold in front of your eyes through a series of creative archetypal expressions?

This type of experience could amount to providing someone new to astrology with a non-verbal archetypal expression of their chart, and you could have them pay attention to any of the characters or scenes that really stick out for them. Perhaps they will be drawn to an expression of energies that they are struggling with or trying to get a better understanding of.

Stanislav Grof is one of founders of transpersonal psychology, and he has said that, "I have come to regard astrology, particularly transit astrology, as the long-sought 'Rosetta stone' of consciousness research, particularly an essential key for understanding the nature and content of holotropic or non-ordinary states of consciousness, both spontaneous and induced."[8]

It could eventually be possible to generate the content of a shamanic journey within virtual reality that reflects someone's inner dynamics that are playing out based upon their astrological configurations and outer planet transits.

Another trend within the virtual reality space is neurogaming, which is the concept of measuring and incorporating biometric information like heart-rate or the galvanic skin response into the VR experience as a feedback mechanism. Imagine being able to measure whether or not someone is experiencing a moment of intensity, and then looking at eye tracking information to determine which archetypal input was correlated with that. You could use this type of visceral feedback to be able to dial up or dial down specific aspects of a VR experience. From an astrological perspective, this would enable you to hone into the fine nuances of a specific archetypal dynamic, and then use that information to go down a fractal rabbit hole exploring other aspects of that archetypal complex.

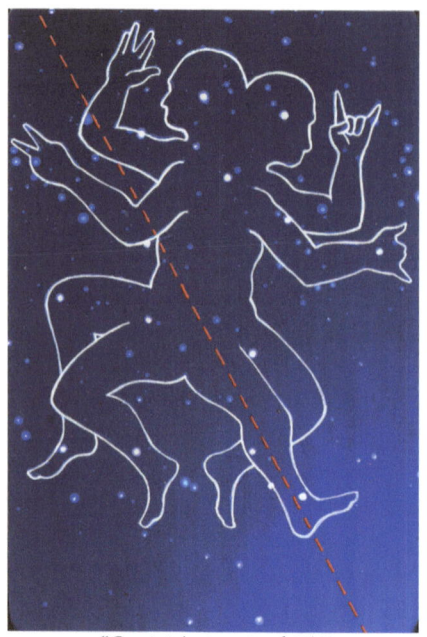
"Gemini (re-imagined #1),"
Acrylic on canvas on board, by Jeff Mihalyo,
for the Constellation *art show*

Doing Retrospective Transit Biographical Research

Doing retrospective work is a key component for being able to understand your historical relationship to archetypal energies so that you can better describe the quality of time in the present moment or into the future.

One of the challenges of doing this retrospective work is to correlate what was happening in your life with these specific moments in time. So there could be a number of things you could do to help craft this historical timeline of your past. You could first list out important dates and times that you can use to search for important astrological correlations.

If you are going the other way of starting with exploring what was happening with big transits from your past, then you could upload a series of photographs with timestamps that help you remember that time in your life. There could also be a set of pop culture references that are pulled in such as the number one movie in the box office, or memorable news events like the Oklahoma City bombing or the death of Princess Diana.

If this type of multimedia information were available within the context of your astrology program, then it might be an interesting and fun way to do this type of retrospective astrological research on yourself.

Astrological Research and Historic Tours

The mouse and keyboard have been the primary method of human-computer interaction for over forty years until the advent of the iPhone and multi-touch screens. Virtual reality has the potential to innovate new types of user interactions such as gesture controls and physical magnetic controllers that enable 3D multi-touch interactions. Keyboard input is also not ideal, and so voice recognition for natural language processing will make it easy to talk to your computer to have it perform an action or input data.

All of these new input methods will provide more intuitive interfaces for interacting with computers, and I expect that it could make it easier and more fun to do astrological research.

Imagine if there were easy ways to annotate specific planetary aspects, and then store them within a database of annotations that you could easily pull up and show right next to an existing chart that you are exploring. Imagine that it was easy to share your annotations with others and that there could be a more rigorous peer review process that could correct mistakes, but also foster more collaboration and innovation.

Just as people surf the web through hypertext links, then imagine taking an immersive historical tour through various key moments in history based upon the diachronic and synchronic archetypal patterning. You could also include the natal charts and transits of important biographical figures relative to significant mundane events. There could be integrations with the astro databank and Wikipedia where it would not only be easy to pull up a famous person's birth information, but you could do searches for specific aspects in a natal chart or mundane charts.

Virtual Reality as One of the Most Social Platforms

When Facebook bought Oculus for $2 billion, founder Mark Zuckerberg said, "Oculus has the chance to create the most social platform ever, and change the way we work, play and communicate."[9] This may seem counter-intuitive at first considering that wearing a VR head-mounted display blocks out your entire view of reality and appears to be very socially isolating. But social interactions within VR can be very realistic and engaging because the head-tracking combined with gesturing is able to convey a lot of body language cues.

Some of the more compelling VR experiences right now are the social experiences such as live talk shows, Karaoke nights, and meet-ups within virtual reality. I foresee a number of virtual meet-ups and virtual conferences that are able to connect astrologers and astrological enthusiasts from around the world. The settings will not be in boring rooms, but rather these will be taking place within outer space and inside of Immersive Astrology programs. Individual astrological practitioners will be able to give readings to people while stepping through their charts, and it will be possible for astrologers to give guided tours, do virtual skywatching and even teach classes through this technology.

Crytpocurrencies like Bitcoin will continue facilitate the growth of virtual economies, and provide an easy way to sell your astrological services to people around the world.

Integration of Various Branches of Astrology

One of the biggest trends in astrology is the recovery of ancient Hellenistic and Medieval techniques, but also a trend towards fusing the insights of everything from modern psychological astrology, evolutionary astrology to even Vedic/Indian and Chinese astrology.

At the moment, these astrological techniques are segregated by specialized software, but I foresee that astrological programs in the future will be able to help with this fusion by implementing the most popular and effective techniques from each branch of astrology. And within a virtual environment where screen real estate is not limited, then it will be easier and easier for astrologers to find patterns and correlations with these techniques, but also be able to collaborate and share insights with each other within these social spaces.

Sacred Sites and Viewing Astrology from Different Points on Earth

There will be a lot of opportunities for going to any point of the planet in VR, and seeing what the night sky looks like there. Not only at this moment in time, but at any point in history where you could observe major astrological configurations.

One of the biggest insights for what engages people within virtual worlds like Minecraft and Second Life is being able to contribute your own creations that other people can experience and enjoy. Virtual Reality will unlock the creative potential in people in terms of creating innovative spaces and recreating sacred sites where people can gather for social experiences or use as the setting for their own astrological research, guided tours, or personal VR experiences.

Institutions like the Smithsonian are also in the process of digitizing their collection of over a hundred and fifty million items, and they are considering making 3D models for some of these objects available for use. So imagine having access to the world's complete collection of cultural heritage artifacts, and how these could be assigned archetypal associations and used within immersive astrology experiences.[10]

Gamification of Astrology

The gaming industry is what is driving the development of virtual reality right now, because they are the ones who have developed the tooling and methods for creating virtual worlds. Game engines like Unity or Unreal Engine 4 are the backbone for creating not only VR games, but they are becoming the de facto standard for how the education, medical and entertainment industries are creating VR experiences.

So it makes sense to think about how to gamify astrology in order to be able to appeal to these early adopters, but also to make the process of learning astrology more fun. There could be everything from real-time strategy games that are scored by how well you elected the time to make an action, to memory games for learning rulerships and dignities, to games identifying where planets are located in space, to a Dr. Who time traveling adventure game that uses astrology to travel back in time to key historical events.

The possibilities here are rich, and I predict that there will be some really compelling experiences that customize the VR gameplay based upon someone's astrological data.

Dressing up your Avatar for Each Planet

Identity and embodiment through avatars is a key component to virtual worlds, and so imagine what it would be like to have an avatar for each of your planets. How would the sign and house placement affect how you dress up your avatar? And what would it be like to be able to walk around a virtual environment and interact with other people as you were dressed up as this planet? This could be a powerful way for connecting to all parts of your astrological identity.

Conclusion

As you can see, the world of VR presents astrologers with a number of new ways to experience astrological signatures, and to explore the dynamics of a natal chart and how it changes over time. VR will help astrologers to recover the third dimension of the night sky that has been lost to the convenience of compressing a 3D world onto a 2D plane. For the first time ever, we will be able to finely control the input to our perceptual system and this has huge implications for what type of experiences we will be able to create and share with each other.

Experiencing the latest virtual reality technology has convinced me that VR will be an unstoppable force that will change everything. *WIRED* recently declared on their cover that VR will "change gaming, movies, TV, music, design, medicine, sex, sports, art, travel, social networking, education—and reality."[11] Let's add astrology to this list. It may sound like hyperbole, but if you look at how the Internet and mobile computing have changed society over the past twenty years then it is not an understatement to say that VR could make as big of an impact if not more. A guiding principle in this time of looking at what could be a revolutionary breakthrough technology is Amara's Law, which states "We tend to overestimate the effect of a technology in the short run and underestimate the effect in the long run." In the short-term, there are great expectations for the potential of VR. In the long-run, I think it is very true to say that VR has the potential to become the most important technology of the history of mankind, as Oculus Rift inventor Palmer Luckey has stated.[12] I suggest, as well, that virtual reality will fully revolutionize the world of astrological practice, paving the way for a truly immersive astrology.

"Scorpio," by Ken Dougherty, for the Constellation *art show*

Endnotes

1 Sébastian Kuntz, "Immersive Virtual Reality," (23 November 2010), slide #7: http://fr.slideshare.net/SebKuntz/immersive-virtual-reality [Accessed 10 August 2014]

2 Mel Slater, "Place Illusion and Plausibility Can Lead to Realistic Behaviour in Immersive Virtual Environments," *Philosophical Transactions of the Royal Society* B, 364, no. 1535 (12 December 2009): pp. 3549–57; http://www0.cs.ucl.ac.uk/staff/m.slater/Papers/rss-prepublication.pdf [Accessed 10 August 2014]

3 Sébastian Kuntz, "A Definition of VR," (17 May 2010): http://cb.nowan.net/blog/a-definition-of-vr/ [Accessed 10 August 2014]

4 Yao *et al.*, "Oculus VR Best Practices Guide," (23 July 2014): http://static.oculusvr.com/sdk-downloads/documents/OculusBestPractices.pdf [Accessed 10 August 2014]

5 Eric Hodgon, "Eric Hodgson on spatial perception, redirected walking & the split between Old VR vs. New VR," *Voices of VR Podcast* #2 (13 May 2014): http://voicesofvr.com/?p=44 [Accessed 10 August 2014]

6 Zachary M. Seward, "Virtual Reality Headset Oculus Rift Meets the Bloomberg Terminal," (9 June 2014): http://qz.com/218129/virtual-reality-headset-oculus-rift-meets-the-bloomberg-terminal/ [Accessed 10 August 2014]

7 Ian Cheney, "The City Dark Press Kit" (11 March 2011): http://www.thecitydark.com/downloads/City_Dark_2011_Press_Kit.zip [Accessed 10 August 2014]

8 Stanislav Grof, "Holotropic Research and Archetypal Astrology," *Archai: The Journal of Archetypal Cosmology* 1, no. 1, (Summer 2009): pp. 50–66: http://www.archaijournal.org/05_Archai_Grof_Holotropic_Research.pdf [Accessed 10 August 2014]

9 Mark Zuckerberg, "Facebook to Acquire Oculus," (25 March 2014): http://newsroom.fb.com/news/2014/03/facebook-to-acquire-oculus/ [Accessed 10 August 2014]

10 Isabel Meyer, "Isabel Meyer on digitizing Smithsonian collections & making them available for educational use," *Voices of VR Podcast* #65 (26 July 2014): http://voicesofvr.com/?p=638 [Accessed 10 August 2014]

11 Peter Rubin, "The Inside Story of Oculus Rift and How Virtual Reality Became Reality," (June, 2014): http://www.wired.com/2014/05/oculus-rift-4/ [Accessed 10 August 2014]

12 James Brightman, "Oculus: VR 'one of the most important technologies in the history of mankind,'" (6 February 2014): http://www.gamesindustry.biz/articles/2014-02-06-oculus-vr-will-be-one-of-the-most-important-technologies-in-the-history-of-mankind [Accessed 10 August 2014]

Kent Bye is an astrologer based out of Portland, OR. He hosts several podcasts, including The Voices of VR Podcast, which features the pioneering game developers, enthusiasts and technologists surrounding the resurgence of virtual reality. Bye is the game designer for Shadow Projection, a virtual reality game developed with two others in 48 hours as part of the Global Game Jam. He has a background in video production and is interested in immersive educational experiences, mindfulness-based applications, and exploring esoteric topics in Virtual Reality. He has also conducted over a hundred interviews with astrolgoers on the Esoteric Voices podcast.

Constellation: The Cosmos, *Artfully Captured*
by Yvette Endrijautzki

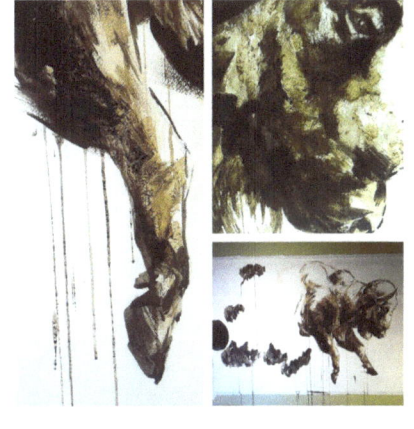

Planets, stars, gods, deities, mysterious celestial bodies, and encrypted symbols; a stupendous enigma, submerged in oblivion and yet so familiar, echoing within the innermost chambers of our genetic encyclopedia. These unfathomable archetypes salute us like messengers, whispering in our ear, allowing us to look deep into the past and towards the future, thereby guiding us through the present.

Astrology is an excellent means to determine auspicious timing for taking action, as in the plays of Shakespeare, where various characters have foreseen their fortune and demise spelled out in their stars. The maxim, "As Above, So Below" speaks about a direct relationship between the activities of the planets, and human activity on earth. These archetypal themes provide the perfect inspiration for The Enlightenment Cabinet: a wandering art exhibit facilitated by artist and curator, Yvette Endrijautzki.

"An Ouverture to the Zodiac"— An exhibit conceived with the idea to let each artist construe and depict their own vision of the twelve zodiacal signs, along with their ruling planets and deities. Each zodiac sign is represented by over 45 various sculptors, painters, mixed media artists, and photographers from all over the world. The exhibit features Seattle artists, alongside representatives from Ohio, Los Angeles, Nevada City, Point Arena, Montana, Paraguay, Tokyo, Berlin, Minneapolis, Spain, Tacoma, France, and many other lines of latitude.

Featured Artists include: Benjamin Vierling, Jeff Mihalyo, Tokyo Jesus,

Yuko Ishii, Julie Baroh, Nick Gucker, Bryan K. Ward, Elizabeth Sheets, Olivier Villoingt, Nathan Cartwright, EGO, Isaac Stuart, Scott Falbo, Larkin, Corey Urlacher, Samuel Araya, Joe Vollan, William Kiesel, J.P Farquar, Carlos Melgoza, Kristina Cyr, Worm Morphology, S.L.Baumgart, Allison & Rachel Pegoraro, Michelle-Smith Lewis, Aaron Jasinski, Chris Summerville, Lara Watson, Javier S. Ortega, Braden Duncan, Ken Dougherty, Anne O'Neill, Kevin E Buntin, Jameson Hubbard, Stephanie Battershell, Jason Middelton, Michael S.Williams, Elijah Evenson, Shiloah Reina, Rich Hall, Kaska Niemiro, Tobi Nussbaum, Wesley Wozniak, Brian White, Zeb Shaffer, Kat Houseman and Yvette Endrijautzki.

"An Overture to the Zodiac" opened at the True Love Gallery on March 13th, and ran until April 6th, 2014. The gallery is a unique shop in the heart of Capitol Hill, borne from the unconventional spirit of the prolific local tattoo and arts community, and is owned by Boris Erickson, Mike Gilmore and George Long. Housed in a 1500 square-foot hybrid gallery/studio space, its walls feature art exhibits curated by in-house and guest curators. After its premier at the True Love Gallery, The Zodiac Show then wandered off for a two month exhibit in April and May at the FULCRUM Gallery on Hilltop in Tacoma, owned by artist Oliver Doriss.

Where the show may travel next is foretold in the ever-shifting patterns in the stars.

www.ingramcontent.com/pod-product-compliance
Lightning Source LLC
Chambersburg PA
CBHW050759110526
44588CB00003B/60